The Weekend Workshop Collection

Birdfeeders, Shelters and Baths

Birdfeeders, Shelters & Baths

by
Edward A. Baldwin

A Garden Way Publishing Book

STOREY

Storey Communications, Inc.
Schoolhouse Road
Pownal, Vermont 05261

The name Garden Way Publishing is licensed to Storey Communications, Inc., by Garden Way, Inc.

Copyright© by Edward A. Baldwin

Printed in the United States by Crest Litho

First Printing 1990

Library of Congress Cataloging-in-Publication Data

Baldwin, Edward A.
  Birdfeeders, shelters & baths: over 25 complete step-by-
step projects for the weekend woodworker/Edward A.
Baldwin.
    p.   cm.
  ISBN 0-88266-625-8 — ISBN 0-88266-623-1 (pbk.)
    1. Birdfeeders — Design and construction.   2. Birdhouses —
Design and construction.   3. Birdbaths — Design and
construction.   4. Woodwork.   I. Title   II. Title: Birdfeeders,
shelters & baths.
QL676.5.B197   1990
690.8'9 — dc20

This book is dedicated to Jessica and Whitney who, like little birds, will someday leave their nest. Hopefully when they try their wings they will have had adequate training with all of the good messages. Also, when they try their solo flights, may they have none of the shackles nor burdens that might stop them from soaring to the highest point in their quest for happiness, success and contentment.

Contents

Acknowledgments

Technical Consultant: Peter Lippincott
Photography: Ed Baldwin and Associates
Typesetting and Layout: A World Of Graphics
Project Construction: D. J. Olin and Ed Baldwin
Art: Jerri Long, Ev Harlow
Project Materials: Hickson Corp., Wolmanized Extra™
Decorative Folk Art: Glennda Suter
Editor: Barbara Kremer

The projects in this book were made using a Shopsmith™ and hand held power tools from Black and Decker™. The router bits and saw blades that we used were Freud™ products.

INTRODUCTION

Attracting wildlife to our homes and property can be a very difficult task. Few wild creatures view mankind as a very safe creature to be around. Birds, on the other hand, are all around us. Depending on the season and the habitat, you are apt to see a wide variety of these little winged creatures hopping and flying about. Creating the right environment, however, is all important to keeping the little critters hanging around. Birds, just like mankind, seek shelter, security, food and water. You can help birds survive and keep them in the neighborhood by just providing these basic items.

HOW TO ATTRACT BIRDS TO YOUR YARD

Putting out birdseed is but one way of attracting birds to your backyard. They have other requirements as well. Plants, shrubs and trees provide places to build nests and are a source of food and security as well. One thing to offer is something the birds may have difficulty in finding themselves. In the southwest this might be water, in the plain states, trees. Planting flowers, vines, shrubs and flowering trees provide seeds and fruit that sustain the birds in the summertime. Did you know that they also need help in the winter time with lodging as well as food? Roosting houses are much different from birdhouses which the birds use in the summer months. The important thing is to remember that you need to do a variety of things to help the birds make it through the year. For example a pyracantha has fruit/ berries that help birds make it through the winter. Providing dense shrubbery that protects the birds from the cold winds is another. Keeping the local "tom cat" at bay is always a problem. Controlling other creatures that rob the birdfeeders or the nests of young birds is still another problem. These are some of the things you have to deal with in creating the right habitat to attract birds to your back yard. On the other hand, by combining the right shrubbery, plants and flowers you also add value to your property so you are doing a lot more than just creating the atmosphere and habitat that birds need to survive.

THE KINDS OF FOOD BIRDS NEED

Birds like a wide variety of foods from the ordinary store-bought bird seed to peanut butter, suet, crackers and french fries. They love a shish-kabob made up of orange and apple pieces and stuck in the corner of a tree. Do you like leftover biscuits and donuts? Birds do, and believe it or not they even eat mashed potatoes.

Roosting houses give shelter in the winter months

Birds, especially the smaller varieties have a very high metabolic rate and have high energy needs. They have to eat foods equivalent to almost 40 to 75 percent of their body weight each day, just to survive. A human being weighing 175 lbs. would have to eat from 75 lbs. to 130 lbs. of food each day just to keep up with a Jenny Wren. Despite the notion that birds will eat a wide variety of foods, they usually stick with their favorite before moving onto the second choice. So, be cautious about putting out a bunch of things that may get ignored. The best choice is to offer a narrow variety of seeds and have several different kinds of birdfeeders for each variety. Mixing your own blend of cracked corn and buckwheat with millet and sunflower seeds is another option if you only have one feeder.

Suet is hard fat trimmed from beef and lamb. Birds love it plain or you can cook it down and add other things to it along with seeds and fat left over from cooking. This is an especially tasty item when mixed with peanut butter and seed varieties. Be certain to only offer suet in the fall and winter months when the temperatures drop since this food will turn rancid quickly in the summer sun.

Some insect-eating species such as nuthatches, chickadees and woodpeckers need suet to replace the insects they can't find in the winter months. Nuts are another important source of energy. Blue jays can be taught to come to your hand for a handout of whole peanuts. Remember that squirrels love peanuts also.

KEEPING PREDATORS AND INTRUDERS AT BAY

Birds need security, a sanctuary where they don't have to be constantly on guard worrying about cats, snakes, raccoons and other prowlers of the night. Putting metal foilers around the bottom of a tree will help keep out most of the raiders. Keeping your grass cut is going to discourage snakes. Put a bell on the cat's collar and use metal foilers around the bottom of feeders and nesting box posts. A metal pole with grease on it is certain to discourage most would-be predators.

Keeping the squirrels out of the birdfeeders is a whole different matter. These little rodents can get around most attempts to keep them away. If you hang feeders from tree branches, make certain you do not use rope to suspend the feeder. Squirrels are bright little creatures. They know to chew through rope. Use wire or chain and then add a foiler or a baffle in

the form of a metal pie pan halfway down the feeder. The best way I know to keep squirrels away from feeders is to build a squirrel feeder with easy access and keep it filled with cracked corn or some other grain. Build the birdfeeder with lots of foilers, make it hard to get at and chances are the squirrels will stay in their part of your yard.

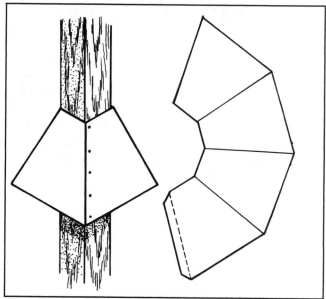

THE GOOD BIRDS AND THE NOT SO GOOD

Some birds, no matter how pretty they are, no matter how cute and nice to see, are a pain to have around. Swallows or chimney swifts like to build nests in chimneys. This can cause fires and smoke problems when you start up the fireplace in the winter. Be certain to add screening to the top of your chimney to discourage them from building nests there. The plus side of this species is that they eat tons of insects, especially mosquitos. English sparrows will build nests anywhere, including your attic if they can get to it. They also have to be discouraged from occupying other birds' homes. They will usually be early occupants so you can clean out their nests in time for the intended species to use. All aggressive birds will monopolize a birdfeeder which can discourage the more timid variety of bird from trying your snacks. Sparrows usually avoid hanging feeders. Feeders with narrow openings will discourage blue jays. Fill your feeders at different times of the day. Blue jays and starlings usually eat later in the day. The titmouse and other smaller birds will usually eat earlier in the day.

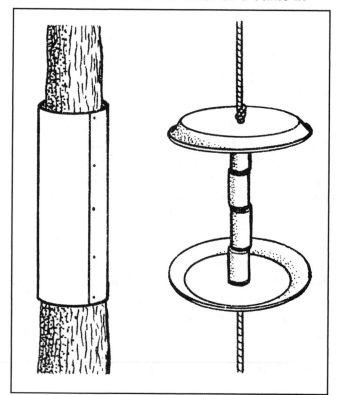

CONSTRUCTION TIPS AND POINTERS

When you place anything outside it is going to have to either stand up to the elements or fall apart, one of the two. It is very discouraging to go to the effort to make something only to see it deteriorate after a few years outside. Today we have access to all kinds of good lumber products designed to deal with the elements. We have hardware with special treatments that can last for 10 or 20 years in the rain and snow. There are new chemicals which resist weathering and rot and take very little maintenence. Knowing which to use to make the project last is what this section is all about.

Wood products for birdfeeders

Several varieties of wood products last in the weather. Redwood, western cedar and cypress are some of the more common. Pressure-treated lumber is also designed for exterior use. All of these woods will, in time, deteriorate if not properly sealed from the elements. Another wood product called Wolmanized Extra™ is pressure-treated lumber that has also been treated to resist the effects of constant exposure to water. It has even been used for watering troughs for horses and cows. We have used this product to build many of the projects contained in this book.

Wood preservatives and finish chemicals

There are oil based and water based types of stains. Normally the term alkyd refers to oil based products and acrylic refers to water based products. Of the two, acrylic is the longer lasting and easier to apply and clean up. You want to apply a product that will soak into the wood and swell into the wood pores and grain and fill the wood fibers, thus providing a lasting sealer/finish. Ordinary house paint will generally not do this. A preparation chemical has to be applied first. The products I prefer are Thompsons water seal, Watco's Natural Exterior Wood Finish and Varathane's Natural Oil Finish. Spar varnishes also can be used but generally do not provide the same amount of protection as the other products I mentioned.

Hardware, fasteners, glue and miscellaneous

Galvanized metal products have long been the favorite for exterior use. I use Dacrotized screws for holding all exterior projects together. This is a coating that doesn't chip or flake as galvanized products sometimes do thus contaminating the wood with black marks after a season in the rain. Never use untreated screws or other hardware items for exterior projects, they rust quickly. Brass or aluminum are the products of choice. Zinc coated products can also be used but won't last as long as the others.

Exterior glue products include epoxy (very expensive), waterproof glues, a variety of new wonder products and clear silicone. I prefer clear silicone for exterior projects because it not only does an excellent job of holding wood together, it also acts as a caulk at the same time.

You'll need rulers, squares, carbon paper in some cases, assorted sandpaper in most cases, pencils and, of course, if you make mistakes, erasers. You'll also need a knowledge of or source for standard woodworking procedures.

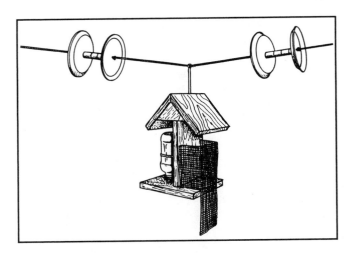

SODA BOTTLE BIRDFEEDER

This birdfeeder is a simple one to make. It is an excellent project for a parent and child to do together. It works best if you hang it right outside your kitchen window where you can see the smaller birds up close while they feed. With minimal tools and less than an hour's time, you can be ready to fill this feeder and wait for the feeding to begin.

MATERIALS

1 piece 1"x½"x6" pine strip
1 piece 1"x2"x6" pine perch support

HARDWARE AND MISCELLANEOUS

1 plastic soda bottle - 2 liter size
2 screw eyes small size
3 brass screws #6, ½" long
Silicone glue
1 piece ¼" wood dowel 4" long

TOOLS REQUIRED

Drill
Heavy scissors
Screwdriver
Coping saw or sabre saw

DIRECTIONS

1. Soak the 2 liter soda bottle in hot tap water. Remove the cover and the plastic bottom. Note: the plastic bottom should come off easily if you fill the bottle with hot tap water to soften the hot melt glue that is used to hold the bottom in place.

2. Cut the bottle to shape as shown, using a heavy scissors. Cut the bottle at the shoulder slightly more than half way leaving an overhanging lip or cowl. This overhang will keep out the rain and protect the birds while feeding.

3. Cut the 1x2 facing in an arc that fits the shape of the bottle. You can use the drawing as shown, but it is best to double check and use the actual size of the opening you have made.

4. Drill a ¼″ hole into the 1x2 facing for the perch. Cut the ¼″ wood dowel to a length of 4″ and glue and insert into the hole.

5. Measure and cut the pine strip to size and position and screw into place using the small screw eyes. Note: it may be necessary to puncture the plastic to get the screws started.

6. Position the 1x2 facing perch out and screw in place using three ½″ #6 brass screws.

7. Hang the feeder from a tree branch using nylon string. Fill with birdseed and sit back and watch the feast begin.

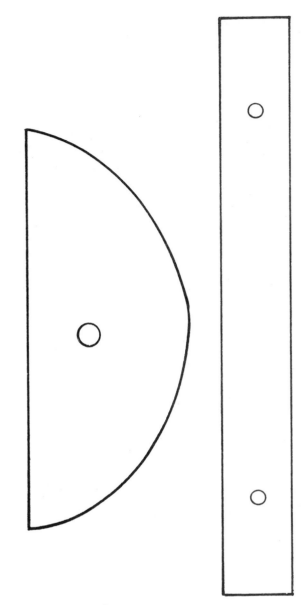

JUICE BOTTLE BIRDFEEDER

You can recycle that bottle that once held held fruit juice, by turning it into a birdseed dispenser. I used a 40 oz Dole® "pure and light" fruit juice jar. Remove the paper label by running the jar under hot water. Add some scrap wood and you have a very functional and nice-to-look-at birdfeeder. This is the kind of project you can do over a weekend with the kids to show the basics of woodworking. Also it provides the opportunity to teach some lessons about helping mother nature's little flying friends.

MATERIALS

1x6 lumber, pressure-treated 36″ long
2 pieces 6″ x 7½″ top and bottom
1 piece 10″ long back
2 pieces ¾″ x ¾″ x 6″ perches
1 piece 3½″ x 6″ center support

HARDWARE AND MISCELLANEOUS

4 pieces ¼″ wood dowel 2″ long
2 cup hooks ½″
6 screws 1½″ Dacrotized
Rubber band or string
Silicone glue
40 oz. juice jar

TOOLS REQUIRED

Drill with 1″ spade bit
Screwdriver
Hammer
Handsaw or sabre saw

DIRECTIONS

You can use any size bottle you may wish. Make certain that you cut the back piece 1″ longer for ease of removing and attaching the bottle to the finished feeder.

1. Measure and cut all of the wood pieces. The center support should be cut to the same diameter as the bottle you choose.

2. Position and attach the center support to the back using glue and screws. I suggest that you pre-drill the holes with a countersink bit.

3. Attach the bottom board to the end of the back board. Place the bottle into position with the rim down onto the bottom board. Trace a pencil mark around the rim of the bottle marking its position on the bottom board, remove the bottle.

4. Remove the bottom board from the back and drill three 1″ holes spaced as shown halfway through the bottom board.

5. Attach the bottom and top boards to the ends of the back board using glue and screws.

6. Measure and cut the ¼″ wood dowel into four pieces 2″ long.

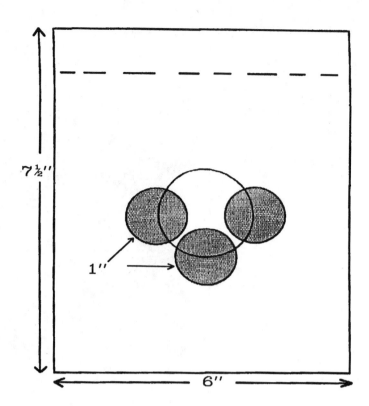

7. Position one of the perch bars against the side of the bottom board and drill two ¼″ holes approximately 1″ from each end of and through the perch bar and ½″ into the bottom board. Repeat this process for the other perch bar.

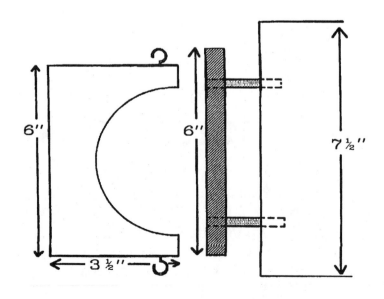

8. Position and glue the ¼″ dowels into place on the bottom board. Attach the perch bars to the ¼″ wood dowels with glue. Allow a 1″ space between the perch bar and the base.

9. Attach ½″ cup hooks to the sides of the center support.

10. Fill the bottle with birdseed and attach it to the feeder, holding it in place with a rubber band or string wrapped around the jar and attached to the cup hooks.

11. Attach the feeder to the side of a building or mount it on a post. Attachment to a metal building would minimize squirrel attacks.

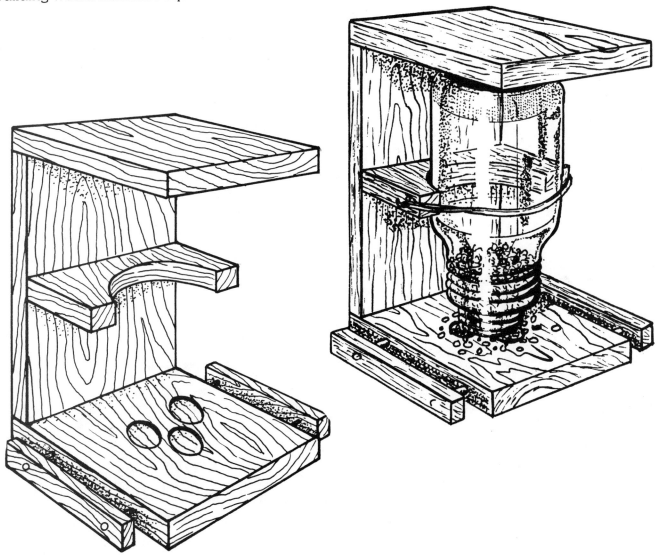

APPLESAUCE BOTTLE BIRDFEEDER

This is an easy weekend project. Take an empty 25 oz. applesauce jar or a Mason jar or the equivalent, mix in a wood frame and you have an attractive and functional feeder. Add some ¼″ hardware cloth and you have a suet dispenser as well. This project can be mounted on a post or old stump or suspended from a tree limb or, for that matter, the rafter of, your front porch.

MATERIALS

1x8 lumber, pressure-treated 36″ long
1 piece 7″ x 8″ base
1 piece 5″ x 9½″ center column
2 pieces 6¾″ x 5½″ roof
2 pieces 3″ x 3″ x 4¼″ roof supports
2 pieces ¼″ thick ¾″ x 4″ bottle/jar support

HARDWARE AND MISCELLANEOUS

8 screws 1½″ Dacrotized or galvanized
2 cup hooks ½″
Silicone glue
Rubber band or string
Staples 5/16″
½″ hardware cloth 10½″x12″
1 jar 25 oz.

TOOLS REQUIRED

Drill with countersink bit
Screwdriver
Hammer
Handsaw or table saw
Stapler
Tin snips

DIRECTIONS

1. Measure and cut all of the wood pieces.

2. Position the center support on the base piece, 3″ from one end. Mark the position with a pencil and drill two holes through the bottom with a countersink drill bit. Attach the center support with two screws and glue.

3. Cut a ⅜″ x ¼″ notch in the center of the jar support pieces so that they overlap forming an "X." Notch the pieces so that the jar rim fits into the notches and is centered over the support.

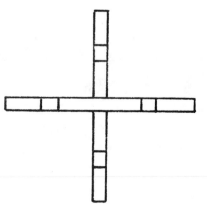

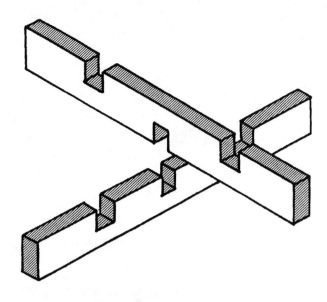

4. Glue and clamp the jar support into position on the base.

5. Cut and bend the suet holder as shown. Be certain to dull any sharp edges.

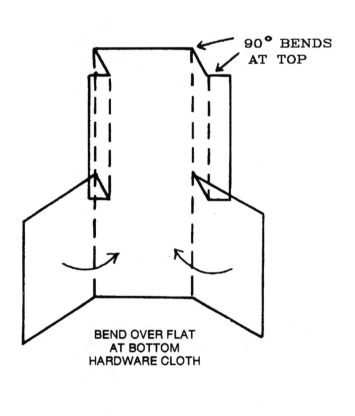

90° BENDS AT TOP

BEND OVER FLAT AT BOTTOM HARDWARE CLOTH

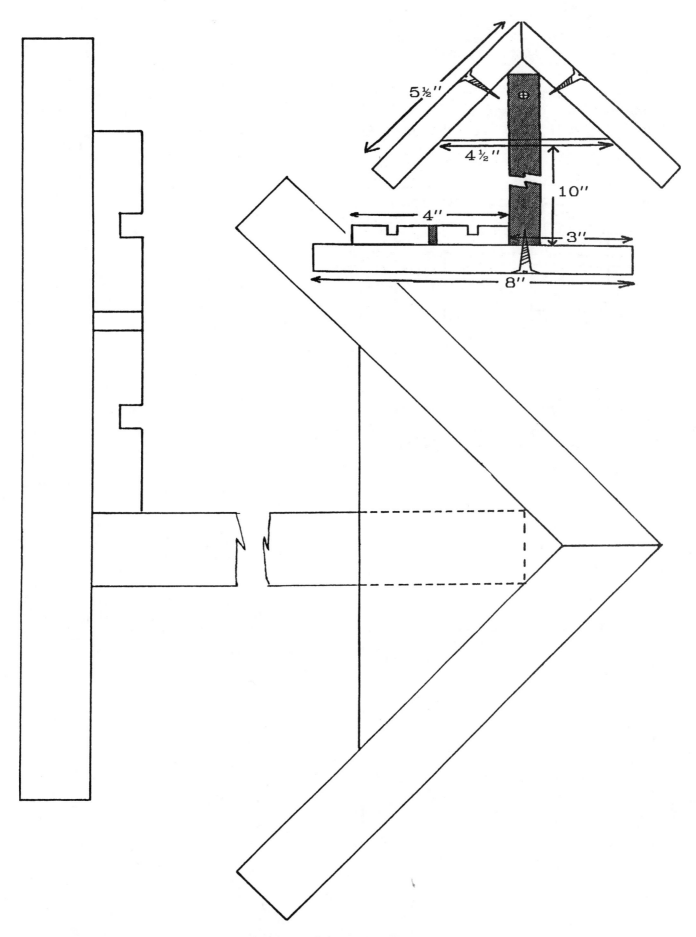

5½"

4½"

10"

4"

3"

8"

6. Attach the roof supports to the center piece using glue and screws. Drill starter holes with a countersink bit.

7. The roof pieces are cut to a 45-degree angle at one end to form the peak of the roof. Attach the roof pieces to the supports using glue and screws.

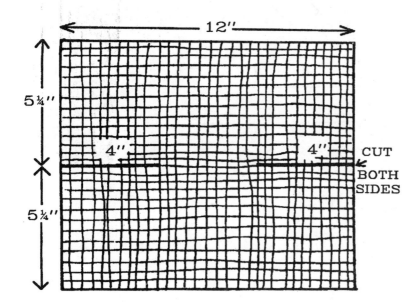

8. Attach the suet cage to the center support, using staples.

9. Attach the cup hooks to the side of the center column on the jar side. Locate them about halfway up the height of the jar.

10. Fill the jar with birdseed and position it on the feeder. Hold the jar in place with a strong rubber band or string wrapped around the jar and attached to the cup hooks. Fill the suet cage and go find a post.

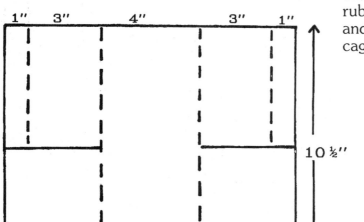

TWO SODA BOTTLE BIRDFEEDER

If your house is like mine and you have teenagers, there is bound to be an empty plastic soda bottle or two lying around. By removing the bottoms and cutting off the necks of the bottles they make great containers for birdseed. By adding a wooden platform to hold the bottles and a roof to keep the feed dry, you have a good looking birdfeeder. This is a very simple project, one the whole family can work on together.

MATERIALS

¾" plywood, pressure-treated
2 pieces 7½" x 17½" roof
1 piece 6½" x 13½" center
1 piece 8¾" x 16" base

2x4 lumber, pressure-treated
1 piece 10" long feed dispenser
2 pieces 2" x 4½" bottle supports
4 pieces 1½" x 1½" x 3¾" roof supports
    need to be cut from piece 4½" long

1x2 lumber, pressure-treated
2 pieces ¼" x 1" x 16" rim front and back
2 pieces ¼" x 1" x 9¼" rim sides

HARDWARE AND MISCELLANEOUS

2 plastic soda bottles - 1 liter size
4 cup hooks ½"
7 screws 1½" Dacrotized
4 screws 2" Dacrotized
4 screws 2½" Dacrotized
2 rubber bands or string
10 wire brads ¾" galvanized
Silicone glue
Adjustable clamps or spring clamps

TOOLS REQUIRED

Drill with countersink bit
Scissors
Screwdriver
Bandsaw, jig saw or coping saw
Hole saw 2½"
Table saw or radial arm saw

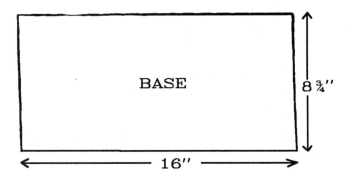

DIRECTIONS

1. Remove the labels and bottoms from the soda bottles by running them under hot water. Fill the bottles with hot water and let them stand for a minute to soften the glue holding the bottoms on, remove the bottoms if desired.

2. Using scissors cut the top of the bottles off so that there is a 1½" opening, set aside.

3. Measure and cut the roof, base and center support from the ¾" plywood stock.

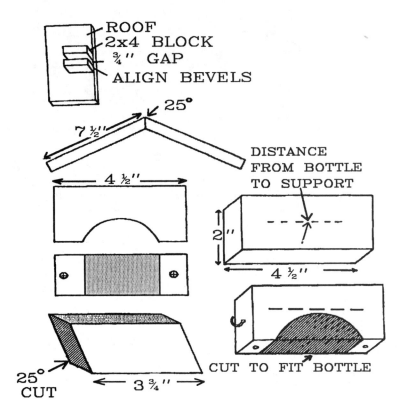

4. Measure and cut the roof supports, bottle supports and feeder dispenser from the 2x4 stock.

5. Using a 2½" hole saw, drill into the ends of the feeder dispenser. Clamp the dispenser firmly and using a sabre saw cut the semicircles in the three sides of each end of the dispenser through which the birdseed will flow.

6. Attach the roof supports to the top of the center piece using glue and 2½" screws.

7. Attach bottle supports to the approximate center of the center support on both sides. Use glue and 2″ screws.

8. Center and attach the dispenser to the base using glue and 1½″ screws.

9. Attach the center assembly to the center of the base over the center of the receptacle. Remember you are screwing into the end grain of plywood, be certain to pre-drill pilot holes with a countersink bit. Use glue and 1½″ screws. It may be necessary to add supports or wedges to keep the center from bending, but we did not do this in the original. If you feel this is necessary, cut small 1½″ triangles from 1″ stock and place on both sides of the dispenser against the bottom of the center assembly. Hold in place with glue and nails.

10. Measure and cut the rim pieces to size from 1″ stock. The size is ¼″ x 1″ x 16″ for the front and back and 9¼″ for the sides. Use wire brads and glue to hold in place, allow a ¼″ lip all around.

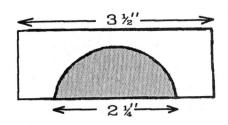

11. Center the roof pieces on top of the center assembly and hold in place with glue and 1½″ screws that are screwed into the roof support pieces.

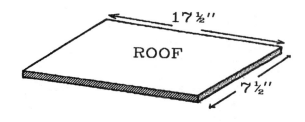

ROOF

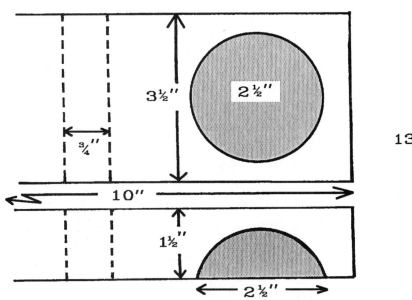

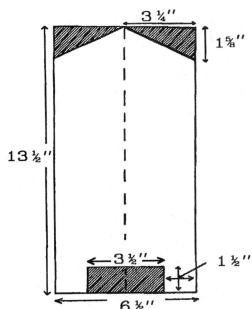

12. Attach cup hooks to the sides of the bottle supports. Fill the bottles with feed and place into position. Secure the bottles with rubber bands or string attached to the cup hooks.

13. Go find a good location for your unique birdfeeder.

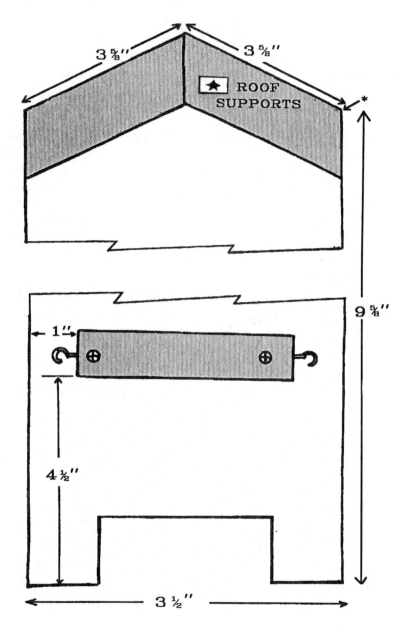

REDWOOD TWO SEED DISPENSER AND SUET FEEDER

This feeder allows you to dispense two types of birdseed, and it also holds suet. This feeder is guaranteed to attract a wide variety of birds to your back yard. Made from a clear piece of redwood 1x12 that is 6 feet long, this project can be easily constructed over a weekend or a couple of nights in the workshop.

MATERIALS

1x12 redwood 72" long
1 piece 9¾" x 20" base
1 piece 4½" x 20" roof back
1 piece 7" x 20" roof front
4 pieces 4" x 10¼" feeder sides
2 pieces 3" x 8" feeder backs
2 pieces 2" x 8" suet feeder supports
2 pieces 3" x 4" roof supports
2 pieces ¼" x 1" x 21" rim front
2 pieces ¼" x 9¾" rim sides

HARDWARE AND MISCELLANEOUS

2   pieces ¼" wood dowel 3" long
2   pieces hardware cloth ¼" grid cut 5" x 8"
2   pieces clear plastic ⅛" cut 3⅝" x 7¾"
40 finish nails #4
16 wire brads 1" long
12 screws 1½" Dacrotized
Wood filler
Silicone glue

TOOLS REQUIRED

Drill with countersink bit
Screwdriver
Table saw or radial arm saw
Stapler
Hammer and countersink
Straight edge
Wire cutters

DIRECTIONS

1. Measure and cut the 1x12 redwood piece as follows:

a. Cross cut one piece 20½" long, rip to 9¾" wide and cut to 20" length. This is the base of the feeder. Use the scrap to cut the rim pieces.

b. Cross cut one piece 20" long and rip one piece 4½" wide at a 45-degree miter. This will be the roof back. Cut the remaining piece to a width of 7". This is the roof front.

c. Measure and cut all of the other pieces to size from the remainder of the 1x12 redwood board.

2. Cut a ⅛" slot ⅜" deep into the facing pieces of the feeder sides, ¼" from the front of the board. This should be done with a table saw or a radial arm saw. This can also be done with a hand held circular saw if you are extremely careful. A router could also be used if you have a ⅛" veining bit. Make certain you book match the sides so when they are facing each other the slots are aligned to also face each other.

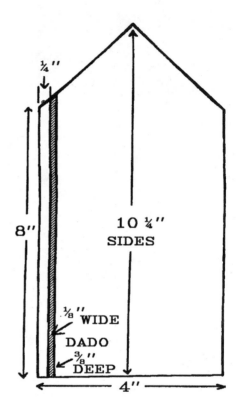

3. Assemble the two seed chambers by attaching the 3" x 8" backs to the sides with glue and #4 finishing nails. Recess the nail heads. Cut the ⅛" plastic to size 3⅝" x 7¾". Slip the plastic into the slots in the sides of each chamber and glue in place using a clear silicone glue. Make certain there is a ½" opening at the bottom for the seed to flow through. Allow the glue to dry thoroughly.

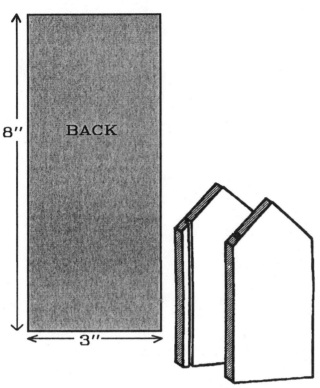

8″

BACK

3″

5. Attach the two suet feeder sides, centered, to the sides of the feed chambers. Cut the hardware cloth to size 5″ x 8″ and staple to the suet feeder side boards.

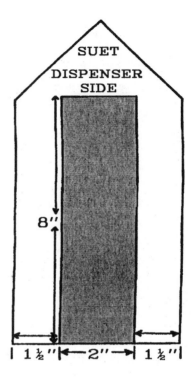

SUET

DISPENSER SIDE

8″

1½″ ←**2″**→ **1½″**

4. Assemble the two roof pieces using glue and four screws. Pre-drill starter holes for the screws using a countersink bit. Let dry thoroughly.

6. Attach the two feeders and the suet feeder assembly to the base board. Center at the back of the board and attach the feeders to the base with glue and screws.

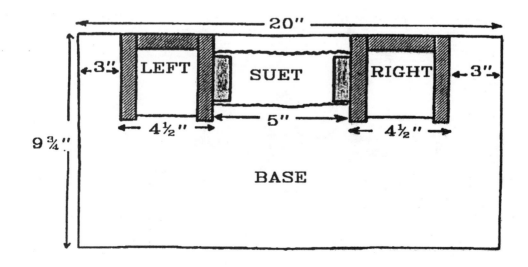

20″

3″ LEFT SUET RIGHT **3″**

9¾″

4½″ **5″** **4½″**

BASE

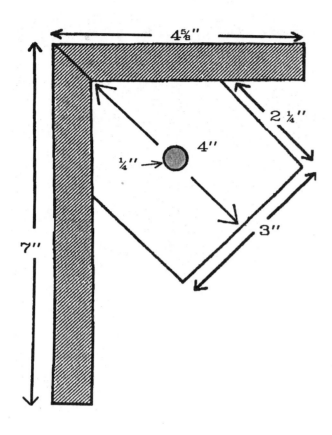

7. Center the roof on top of the feeder assembly. Mark the position for each roof support piece, remove the roof and attach the roof supports using glue and screws. Allow the glue to dry thoroughly.

8. Measure and cut the rim pieces and attach them to the sides, front and back of the base. There should be about a ¼" lip to keep the seed from falling off the edge. Use glue and wire brads to hold the strips in place.

9. Place the roof assembly back on top of the feeders. Using a drill with a ¼" bit drill a hole through the roof support and feeder side on both sides of the roof assembly. Cut a ¼" wood dowel to a 3" length and insert into this hole to keep the roof in place. You may have to sand the dowel a bit to make it fit properly.

10. Seal the project with a quality grade of wood sealer. Go find a post for your feeder, load it up and watch the birds come-a-flying.

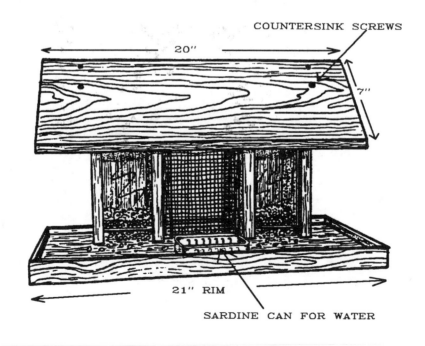

COUNTERSINK SCREWS

21" RIM

SARDINE CAN FOR WATER

THE ROUND BOTTLE FEEDER

This easy to build feeder features an upturned juice bottle with its labels removed as the feed chamber. The seed is released as it is needed. The attractive circular shape can be viewed from all sides. This feeder can be post mounted or hung from a tree limb.

MATERIALS

¾" plywood, pressure-treated
2 pieces 10½" diameter top and base

2x4 lumber, pressure-treated
4 pieces 1" x 1" x 7" posts
1 piece 1/16" x 1" x 36" rim
1 piece 3½" x 3½" feeder
    dispenser/support

HARDWARE AND MISCELLANEOUS

8 screws 1½" Dacrotized
10 wire brads ¾" galvanized
2 screw eyes (optional)
Silicone glue
1 jar 42 oz.

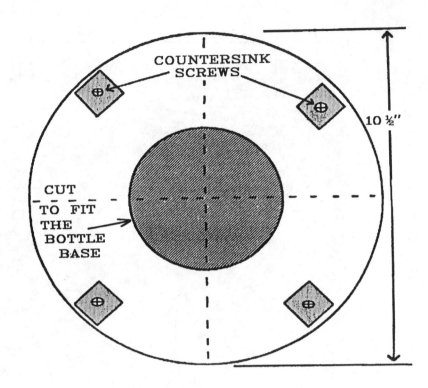

TOOLS REQUIRED

Drill with countersink bit
Screwdriver
Sabre saw or band saw or coping saw
Table saw
Hammer

DIRECTIONS

1. Measure and cut the top and base circles from ¾" pressure-treated plywood. Measure and cut a hole in the center of the top circle large enough to allow the jar to pass through. Ours was 4½". We used a Dole® 42 oz. juice jar as the seed container. Tip: I normally cut holes of this type with a band saw by cutting through the center and then gluing a strip of thin wood in the saw kerf to fill up the void. This is much quicker than drilling a starter hole and cutting out the center with a sabre saw.

2. Measure and cut the four support posts from 2x4 stock. Make them 7" long or long enough so that the bottle you use can just barely stick up from the top. The whole idea is to use the top to support the bottle and keep it from falling over in high winds.

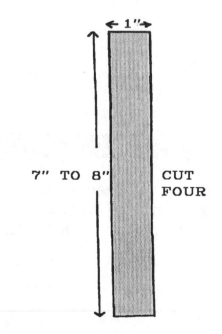

3. Measure and cut a 3½" length of 2x4. Cut two ¾" arcs as shown. You need a band saw or coping saw to do this properly. Next drill a hole through the center large enough to accommodate the mouth of the bottle but small enough to catch the rim or neck and keep it at least ½" off the base. The jar we used had a 2" mouth or rim.

5. Attach the four 1" posts to the base and top using 1½" screws countersunk into the top and base.

6. If you wish to hang the feeder from a tree branch, add two screw eyes large enough to support the weight of the feeder. Tip: Remember to use wire or small chain and put a pie tin baffle halfway up the suspension.

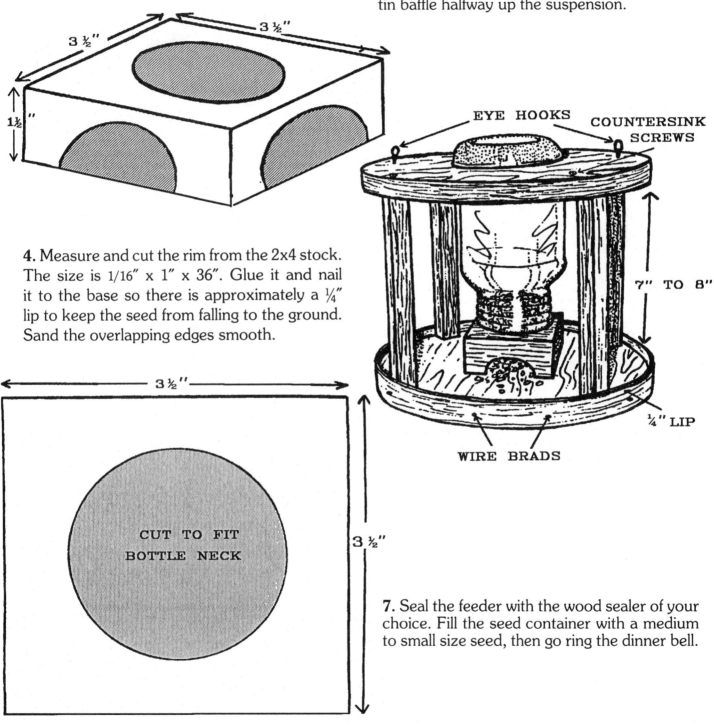

4. Measure and cut the rim from the 2x4 stock. The size is 1/16" x 1" x 36". Glue it and nail it to the base so there is approximately a ¼" lip to keep the seed from falling to the ground. Sand the overlapping edges smooth.

CUT TO FIT BOTTLE NECK

7. Seal the feeder with the wood sealer of your choice. Fill the seed container with a medium to small size seed, then go ring the dinner bell.

TIN CAN BIRDFEEDER

This is a great project for the Boy or Girl Scouts to build as projects for the community. You might want to take your little boy or girl into the workshop this weekend and turn out two or three of these very basic birdfeeders. We got carried away with Swedish tole painting to add a touch of class to this project.

MATERIALS

1x6 pine, pressure-treated 18″
2 pieces 2½″ x 5½″ end braces
1 piece 5½″ x 6″ bottom
1 piece 5½″ x 5½″ back

HARDWARE AND MISCELLANEOUS

¼″ wood dowel 3″ long
4 finishing nails #4
3 flat head screws ¾″
2 deck screws 1½″ Dacrotized
Silicone glue
Paint of your choice
1 tin can 32 oz. size

TOOLS REQUIRED

Drill with countersink and ¼″ drill bits
Screwdriver
Hammer
Sabre or coping saw

DIRECTIONS

1. Prepare the tin can by removing the top completely, washing the can thoroughly and hammering down any sharp metal edges.

2. Cut two pieces from the 1x6, 2½″ long and 5½″ wide. Trace the base of the can (centered) to form a semicircle on the long side of each block. Carefully cut to shape. Save one of the semicircle cut-offs, re-trim it to fit inside the mouth of the tin can.

3. Draw another small semicircle on the piece you saved and cut to shape. Drill a ¼″ hole centered into the piece for the perch. Position this piece in the mouth of the tin can and screw in place using ¾″ flat head wood screws. Pierce the tin can with a nail point and hammer or the tip of the countersink bit so the screws can pass through.

4. Measure and cut a piece of the 1x6, 6″ long. Glue and nail the two pieces from step 2 to the ends of this board. Let the glue dry thoroughly.

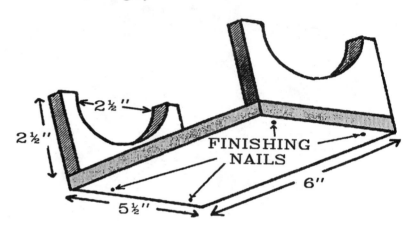

5. Measure and cut the back piece from the 1x6. We used a piece 5½″ long. Attach it to the end of the assembly from above as shown. Use two Dacrotized screws and pre-drill the holes with a countersink bit.

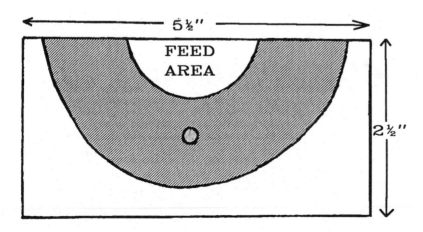

6. Measure and cut a 3″ length of ¼″ wood dowel and glue it into the facing board in the mouth of the tin can.

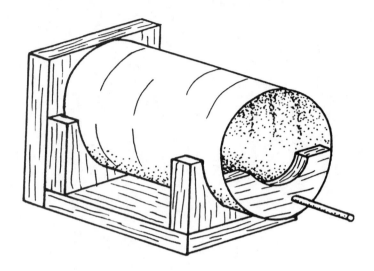

7. Paint the project the color of your choice. At a very minimum, varnish the tin can to retard rust.

8. Load it up with birdseed, set the can in place and go find your favorite birdfeeding spot.

FOUR-STATION BIRDFEEDER

This four-station feeder is designed to hold a lot of seed. It will hold the smallest to the largest seed or grain and is certain to get the attention of birds and squirrels alike. It is designed to be post mounted. If you plant the post far enough away from any trees, cover the post with metal and place a metal bell underneath the feeder, you might get lucky and keep away the pesky squirrels.

MATERIALS

¾" plywood, pressure-treated
2 pieces 20" diameter circles

1x8 pine, pressure-treated
2 pieces 18" long feed chamber
4 pieces 3" x 16" base support
4 pieces 2" diameter and
4 pieces 3½" diameter feed chamber lids/covers
1 piece ¹⁄₁₆" x 1" x 66" base rim

HARDWARE AND MISCELLANEOUS

4 pieces clear acrylic 7" x 11"
20 wire brads ¾" galvanized
20 screws 1½" Dacrotized
Silicone glue

TOOLS REQUIRED

Drill with countersink bit and 2½" circle cutter
Screwdriver
Sabre saw or band saw
Table or radial arm saw
Hammer

DIRECTIONS

1. Measure and cut the top and base from ¾" pressure-treated plywood. Each is 20" in diameter. Cut the four feed chamber openings in one piece using a 2½" hole saw or a sabre saw.

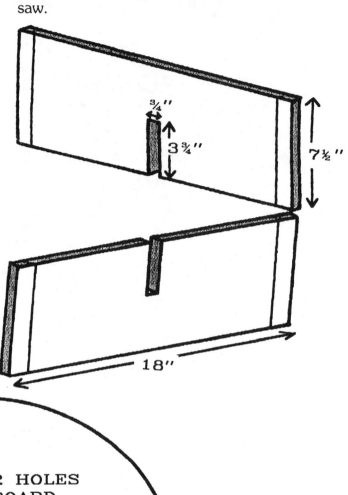

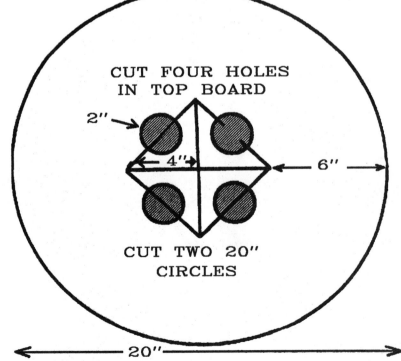

CUT FOUR HOLES IN TOP BOARD

2"

4"

6"

CUT TWO 20" CIRCLES

20"

2. Measure and cut the two pieces of feed chamber walls 18″ long, from the 1x8. Cut a ¾″ x 3¾″ dado in the center of each board.

3. Cut a 45-degree slot in the ends of both sides of the boards from step 2. Set the saw blade to cut a ¼″ deep groove 1¼″ from the edge of each end on both sides of the two boards.

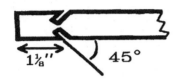

4. Measure and cut four pieces of clear acrylic 7″ x 11″. Be certain to leave the protective coating on the acrylic until after the pieces are cut.

5. Assemble the feed chamber by putting the feed chamber boards together to form an "X." Use glue in the dado slot. Slip the acrylic pieces into the ⅛″ slots and hold in place with clear silicone glue. Make certain there is at least a ½″ opening at the bottom. Allow this assembly to dry thoroughly.

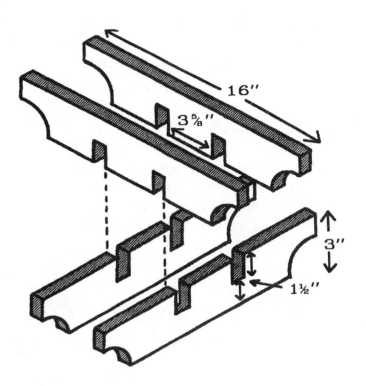

6. Measure and cut the four base support boards from the 1x8. Each piece is 3″ x 16″. Cut a ¼ circle in each end of the boards as shown and cut dados 1½″ deep and ¾″ wide. These are designed to overlap a 4x4 post.

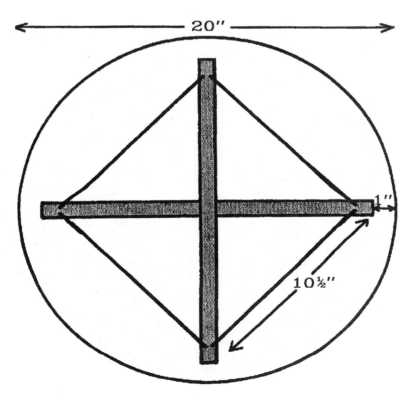

7. Attach the base support assembly to the base with 1½″ Dacrotized wood screws. Attach the feed chamber and the top to this assembly. Use glue.

8. Rip a ¹/₁₆″ strip of wood from the 1x8 wood stock 1″ x 66″. Attach to the base using ¾″ galvanized wire brads. Overlap the ends slightly and trim flush.

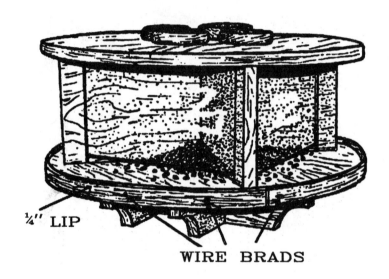

¼″ LIP

WIRE BRADS

9. Measure and cut the four pieces of feed chamber lids from the 1x8 stock. Cut four pieces 2″ diameter and four pieces 3½″ diameter. Center and attach the smaller piece to the larger piece and hold in place with glue and 1½″ screw.

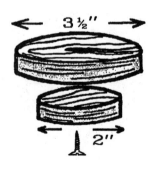

3½″

2″

10. Attach the feeder to a 4x4 post, fill with feed and attach the lids.

WEATHERVANE BIRDFEEDER

This unique feeder always points into the wind and thus keeps the birds safe from the wintery gales. If you need to know which direction the wind is blowing all you have to do is look at your birdfeeder. This project rotates on a small "lazy Susan" bearing assembly that provides good wide support and rotates at the slightest movement of the wind. We painted ours with decorative tole painting that really makes a nice addition to the back yard.

MATERIALS

¾" plywood, pressure-treated
1 piece 10" x 11½" base/bottom
2 pieces 9" x 11½" sides
1 piece 5¼" x 12" front roof
1 piece 9" x 12" roof back
1 piece 6½" x 10" back
2 pieces 6" diameter lazy Susan supports

2x4 lumber, pressure-treated
1 piece 1½" x 1½" chimney
2 pieces ¼" x 1" x 6" rim

1x6 lumber, pressure-treated
1 piece 4¾" x 24" vane
1 piece 2½" x 2½" chimney base
1 piece 2" diameter feed cover
2 pieces 3" x 3⅝"
2 pieces 3" x 5⅛"

HARDWARE AND MISCELLANEOUS

18 screws 1½" Dacrotized
1 piece clear acrylic ⅛" x
    7½" x 10½"
4 wire brads ¾"
Silicone glue
Lazy Susan bearings 4"
4 wood screws 3½" long

TOOLS REQUIRED

Drill with countersink bit,
    ½" and 2" hole cutters
Screwdriver
Hammer
Table saw
Sabre saw or band saw
Router with rounding over bit

DIRECTIONS

1. Measure and cut the bottom, side and back pieces.

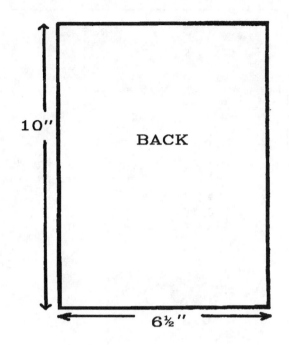

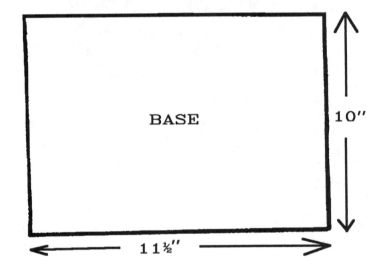

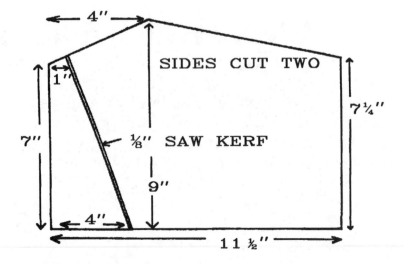

2. Adjust your table saw to a ⅜″ depth of cut and cut the slot as shown into the side pieces for the feed retainer. Make certain the saw kerf is wide enough for the ⅛″ acrylic sheet.

3. Measure and cut the two roof pieces to size. Cut the roof peak to a 25-degree angle.

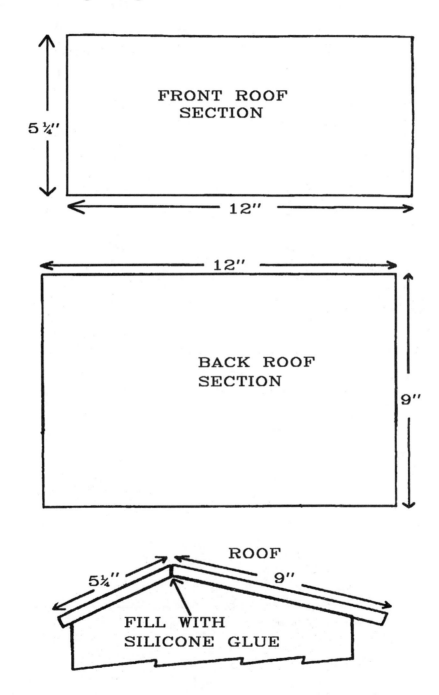

4. Assemble the roof, side bottom and back pieces using silicone glue and 1½″ screws. Drill a 2″ hole in the center upper (top) part of the front roof. Save the cut-out piece.

5. Measure and cut the acrylic sheet to size. Remove the protective coating and insert it into the feed retainer slot in the sides. Hold in place with clear silicone glue. Make certain there is at least a ½″ space at the bottom for the seed to pour through.

6. Draw the vane design onto 1x6 pressure-treated lumber and cut to size. Cut out the heart design; this is an option. Using a rounding over bit, rout the inside heart design and the sides of the vane. Do not rout the part that is attached to the feeder.

7. Attach the vane to the center rear of the feeder box. It should just barely touch the acrylic feed retainer. Use 1½″ screws and silicone glue.

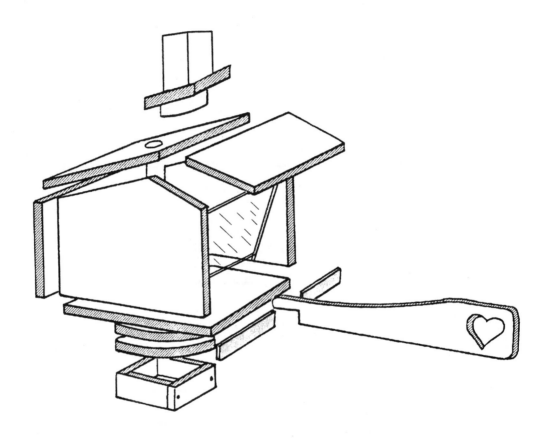

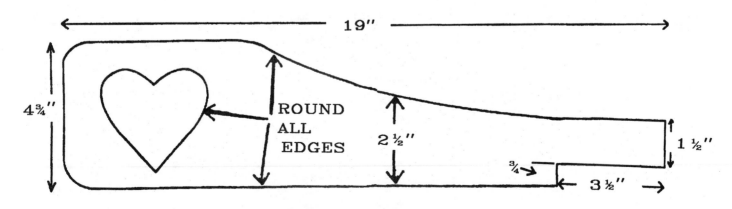

19″

4¾″

ROUND
ALL
EDGES

2½″

¾

1½″

3½″

8. Measure and cut the two support boards for the lazy Susan bearing from ¾" plywood stock. The size is 6" diameter. Attach the lazy Susan bearings in the center of these two boards. Note: you will have to drill a ½" hole through one board to attach both sides of the bearing. This hole should line up with the screw holes on the end of the bearing facing plate.

11. Measure and cut the chimney from 2x4 stock. Measure and cut the chimney base using 1" stock. This along with the circle from step 4 forms the feed chamber cover. Attach all three pieces using glue and one 2" wood screw.

12. Finish the project with the wood sealer of your choice. Go find a post and attach the feeder using wood screws. Make certain it is level or it will not work.

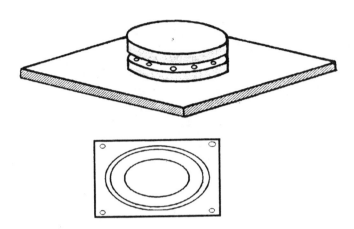

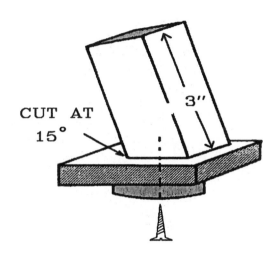

CUT AT 15°

3"

9. Measure and cut the four boards for the post and lazy Susan support, two pieces 3" x 3⅝" and two pieces 3" x 5⅛". Assemble the four pieces using 1½" screws and glue.

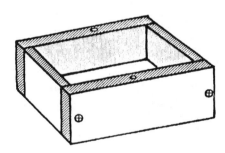

10. Find the center of gravity on the bottom of the feeder and attach the lazy Susan assembly, centered on the bottom of the feeder using glue and 1½" screws. Attach the assembly from step 9 to the bottom of this assembly using 3½" wood screws.

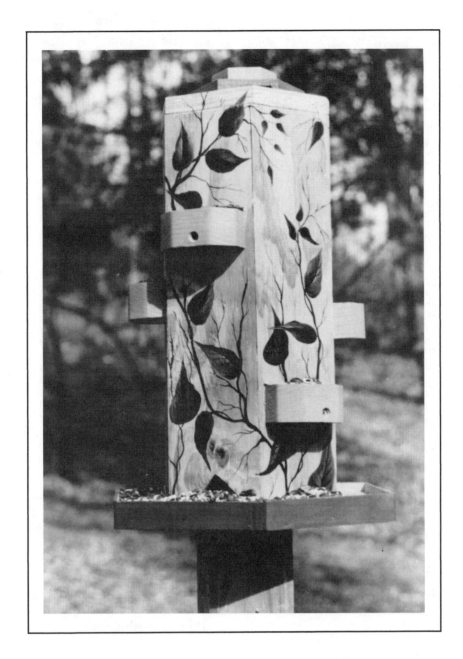

HEXAGONAL BIRDFEEDER

This tall and graceful feeder is actually an eight-station feeder. It is designed to be either post mounted or it could also be suspended from a tree limb provided you used a strong chain. It will hold a large volume of seed. Since there is no roof, we suggest you place it where some overhead protection can keep the feed dry.

MATERIALS

¾" plywood, pressure-treated
1 piece 12¾" hexagon base
1 piece 8" hexagon top
1 piece 5" hexagon lid top
1 piece 2¾" hexagon lid middle
6 pieces 4" x 16" sides
1 piece 2½" diameter lid bottom

2x4 lumber, pressure-treated
6 pieces 1¾" x 3½" feed stations
6 pieces ¼" x 1" x 7" base rims

HARDWARE AND MISCELLANEOUS

7 screws 1½" Dacrotized
7 screws 2" Dacrotized
12 wire brads ¾" galvanized
Silicone glue

TOOLS REQUIRED

Drill with countersink bit,
    1" and 2½" hole cutters
Screwdriver
Hammer
Table saw
Compass
Band saw or sabre saw
Web clamp, rubber bands or rope

DIRECTIONS

1. Measure and cut the six sides of the feed chamber from the ¾" pressure-treated plywood. Cut 4" wide with a 30-degree bevel on each side and 16" long.

2. Drill a 1" hole centered into each of the six side boards. We staggered the position of each hole to give the best look to the feeder. Drill holes in two boards 5" from the top, two boards 5" from the bottom and two boards centered. Cut a shallow V slot in the bottom of the two boards with the center hole.

CUT TWO OF EACH

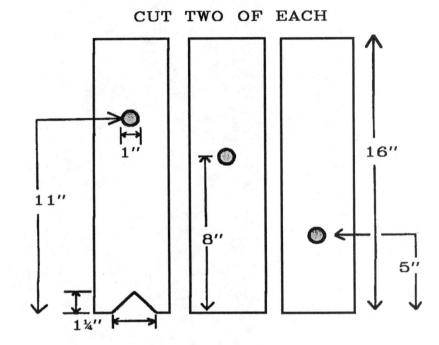

3. Position the boards so that each board with a like hole placement is opposite each other, glue all boards together. Hold in position with a web clamp or rubber bands or rope wrapped around the assembly and drawn tight. Allow this assembly to dry thoroughly.

4. Measure and cut the base and the roof of the feeder from ¾" plywood. Center and attach the base and the roof pieces to the feeder using glue and 1½" screws.

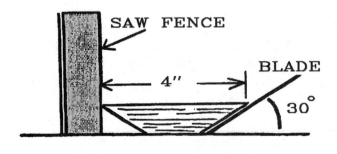

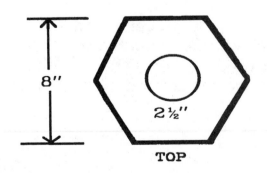

TOP

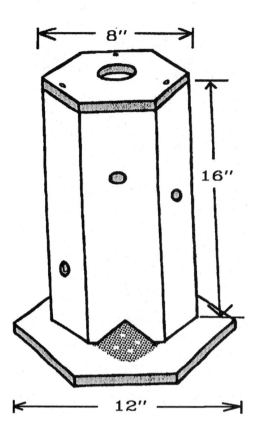

8"

16"

12"

6. Drill a countersink hole in the lower center of each station and attach to the feed chamber sides with a 2" screw. Note: position the stations so the top of the hole in the feed chamber is ¼" above the top of the feed station. This will allow the feed to pour into the opening but not overflow.

7. Measure and cut the three pieces forming the lid assembly and assemble all of the pieces, using glue and a 2" wood screw.

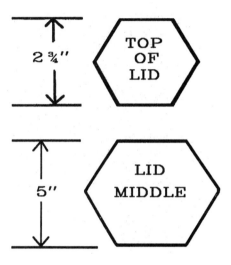

2 ¾"   TOP OF LID

5"   LID MIDDLE

5. The feeder stations are made by drilling 1" holes 1" deep into the center of a 2x4 every 3½" and then ripping the board down the center and cutting the feeder stations to 3½" lengths with the half hole in the center. Cut to shape using a sabre or band saw.

8. Measure and cut the base rim strips from the 2x4 stock and attach to the base using ¾" wire brads and glue. Trim the pieces to fit flush.

9. We decorated the sides of the feeder with painted vines and leaves. Feel free to add your own decorative touches to your finished project.

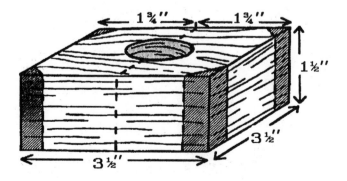

1 ¾"   1 ¾"

1½"

3½"

3½"

WEATHERVANE FEEDER

You'll always know which way the wind is blowing with this unusual feeder.

APPLE SAUCE BOTTLE FEEDER

Even an apple sauce jar can be part of a bird station like this one that includes a suet-cage feeder on its other side.

SWISS CHALET BIRDFEEDER

This project says first class, it is a certain crowd stopper.

POST MULTISTATION FEEDER

As the seed supply dwindles, you'll see the birds only feeding from the lower stations and will know it's time to fill-'er-up.

FLYING SAUCER FEEDER

A two-liter soda bottle mounted on a tray makes this feeder a frequent stopover for your flying friends.

THE ROUND BOTTLE FEEDER

For contrast, making this frame like its container gives an attractive look.

FEEDER PROJECTS FOR LITTLE HANDS
These simple projects can be made by children.

SODA BOTTLE FEEDER

Instead of throwing away that two-liter soda bottle, use it to feed your feathered friends from one of our quickest and easiest projects.

BIRD BATH

We designed this bathing spot to be easily maintained while giving it a look of classic simplicity.

SEMI-SQUIRREL-PROOF FEEDER

Pesky squirrels won't be able to steal seed from this feeder because of its bird-sized entry holes. Protection from the weather is another feature.

COUNTRY STORE FEEDER

Your featured guests will love "shopping" in this country store as much as you will enjoy watching them.

ROOSTING BOX

Birds also need "safe houses" where they can get out of the weather and rest.

TWO SODA BOTTLE FEEDER

Following the principle that two are always better than one, this double feeder gives your little guests two choices from your menu.

JUICE BOTTLE FEEDER

Here's another way to feed the birds with a simple throw-away item, a 40 oz fruit juice bottle, turned upside down and mounted in a frame.

TIN CAN FEEDER

The simplest containers, such as the tin can used here, can be made unique with a little paint creatively applied.

REDWOOD TWO SEED DISPENSER

Three separate compartments give this birdfeeder triple capacity and allow it to attract a wide variety of species to your yard.

HEXAGONAL FEEDER

This six-sided feeder provides plenty of feeding stations and is easy to decorate in a vine and leaf design.

RED DOG SALOON FEEDER

Birds will "belly up" to the seed bar when you open your Red Dog Saloon for business.

SWEETHEART WINDOW FEEDER

This window-ledge design is functional as well as appealing.

SWEETHEART FEEDER

Novelty feeders like this one are fun to make and a pleasure to have in the yard.

MULTISEED FEEDER

A four-station feeder in-the-round allows at least one side to be out of the wind at all times.

BIRD BATH, FEEDER COMBO

We added a very basic bird bath to a tray feeder for this dual-purpose station that will bring you hours of birdwatching pleasure.

GAZEBO FEEDER

Everybody loves a gazebo, and your feathered friends will help you enjoy this one.

RAIN COVER WINDOW FEEDER

The see-through top on this feeder will let you get an even closer look at your visiting seed-eaters.

THE GAZEBO FEEDER

This birdfeeder says, "First Class." Built on a scale to accommodate several birds at a time, it is 16 inches square and almost 2 feet high. The top lifts off so you can pour seed into the center chamber. The latticework is an especially nice touch. With the shingled roof and decorative cornice, this is guaranteed to get the attention of everyone in your neighborhood.

MATERIALS

Note: There is a lot of cutting and ripping and most of the pieces that make up this project are non-standard. If you are a beginner to woodworking take heed.

2x4 lumber, pressure-treated
4 pieces 15″ pole housing
8 pieces 1¼″ x 1¼″ x 9½″ columns
4 pieces 1¼″ x 1¼″ x 15″
 roof supports
4 pieces ⅜″ x 1″ x 11″
 roof edge cover
8 pieces ⅜″ x 1¼″ x 5⅞″ cornices

2x8 lumber, pressure-treated
1 piece 5″ x 5″ and
1 piece 4″ x 4″ seed cover.
70 pieces 3/16″ x 1¾″ x 7¼″ shingles

1x8 lumber, pressure-treated
2 pieces 15″ long base
4 pieces ¾″ x ¾″ x 14″
 feed chamber edges
8 pieces ⅜″ x 5⅞″ and
8 pieces ⅜″ x 5⅛″ lattice top
 and bottom support
16 pieces ⅜″ x 3″ lattice end support
4 pieces ⅜″ x ⅝″ x 5¼″
 roof top molding
4 pieces 3/16″ x ¾″ x 5 ⅜″
 top roof covers
8 pieces 2½″ x 5⅛″ lattice

⅜″ plywood, pressure-treated
4 pieces 15¼″ x 9″ x 4¼″
 roof sides

HARDWARE AND MISCELLANEOUS

20 screws 1½″ Dacrotized
16 screws 1″ Dacrotized
Box finishing nails ½″ galvanized
Box finishing nails ¾″ galvanized
Box ¾″ wire brads

4 pieces clear acrylic ⅛″ x
 4″ x 13½″ feed chamber walls
Silicone glue, caulk gun size
Assorted sandpaper

TOOLS REQUIRED

Table saw
Band saw
Hammer
Drill with countersink bit
Screwdriver
Belt sander

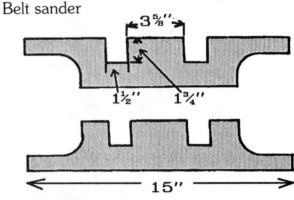

DIRECTIONS

1. Measure and cut the pole housing pieces from the 2x4 stock. Cut a 2″ quarter circle from the ends of all four boards. Cut two 1½″ notches, 1¾″ deep as shown in each board. Allow a space of 3⅝″ in the center so that when assembled a 4x4 post will fit in the center opening (a 4x4 is actually 3½″ square).

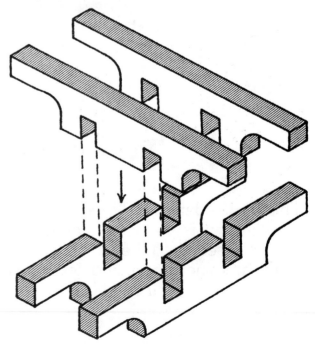

2. Measure and cut two 15″ lengths from the 1x8 stock. Center and glue and screw these boards to the assembly from above. This forms the base of the feeder.

3. Measure and cut the 8 column pieces from the 2x4 stock. Each is 1¼″ square and 9½″ long.

4. Attach the columns to the base using screws and glue. Remember to countersink the screw holes. The columns are placed in each corner with one column centered on each side.

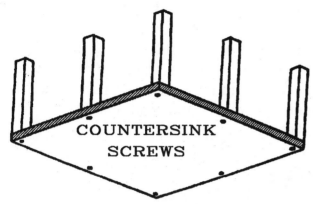

5. Measure and cut the roof supports as shown. Miter each end and attach to the columns using ¾″ finishing nails, screws and glue. Allow to dry.

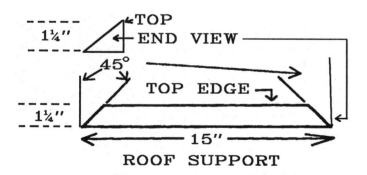

6. Rip about 60″ of 1x8 wood stock ¾″ x ¾″. Lower your table saw blade to a depth of ¼″ and cut a dado the width of the saw blade or ⅛″ into the center of two sides of the wood strip as shown in the illustration. Cut four 14″ pieces from this wood strip for the feed chamber.

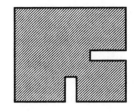

7. Measure and cut four pieces of clear acrylic sheet to size for the feed chamber walls, 4″ x 13½″. Glue the acrylic sheets and the wood strips as shown. Allow at least a ½″ space at the bottom for the feed to pour through. Allow this assembly to dry thoroughly.

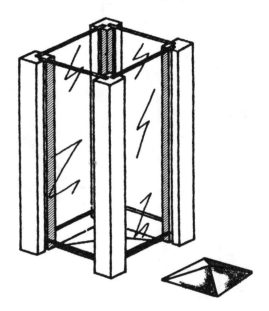

8. Position the feed chamber in the center of the base and glue and toenail with ¾″ wire brads to the base. Option: at this point you may want to put a pyramid shaped wood piece into the center of the feed chamber so that the seed will flow outward. A 1″ rise will work fine. Cut a strip off of a 4x4 or use a 3½″ strip of 2x4.

9. Measure and cut the cornice pieces from 2x4 stock. Cut to shape and then slice to a ⅜″ thickness, make eight. Attach to the top of each opening using ¾″ wire brads and glue.

10. Measure and cut the lattice top and bottom and end supports or railing from the 1x8 wood stock.

11. The lattice is made by first ripping about a 60″ length of 1x8, 2½″ wide. Set your table saw miter gauge to 45 degrees and the blade to a height of slightly over ⅜″. Make multiple passes at ¼″ intervals to cut the lattice slot on one side. Turn the board over and do the

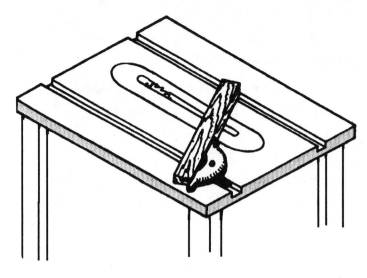

same only reverse the pattern. The width of most saw blades is about ⅛″ so it will be necessary to make two passes for each slot, unless of course you own an adjustable dado blade.

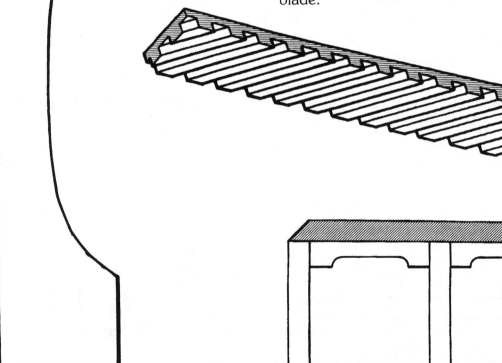

12. Cut the lattice to 5⅛″ and glue and nail it and the railing or support pieces into position using ¾″ wire brads and glue.

13. Measure and cut the roof pieces from ⅜" plywood. Position the pieces onto the roof supports as shown and glue and screw into place using 1" screws. Run a bead of silicone glue the length of each side. Allow to dry thoroughly.

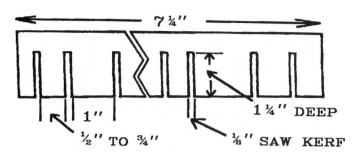

7 ¼"

1"   ½" TO ¾"   1 ¼" DEEP   ⅛" SAW KERF

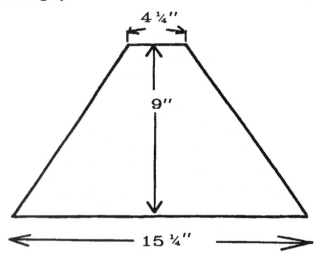

4 ¼"

9"

15 ¼"

14. Using ¾" wire brads toenail the edges of the roof. Sand the edges at the top flat. Note: you can saw the edges before assembling the roof so they are flat at the top. I found sanding to be just as fast.

15. Make the wood shingles as follows. Rip 1¾" lengths from the ends of the 2x8 stock. This is actually 7¼" to 7½" in length. Set your miter gauge on your table saw to 90 degrees and bolt a support board to the miter gauge that will pass through and over the saw blade. Put a small finishing nail into the support board at a 1" distance from the saw blade as a positioning gauge. Set the blade to a height of 1⅛". Cut slots into the wood strips at 1" intervals. You can also make a variation by alternately cutting slots at ½" and ¾" spaces from each other. Caution: make certain you pass through the saw blade and turn the saw off before making each successive cut. Do not draw the support board back through the blade while the motor is running.

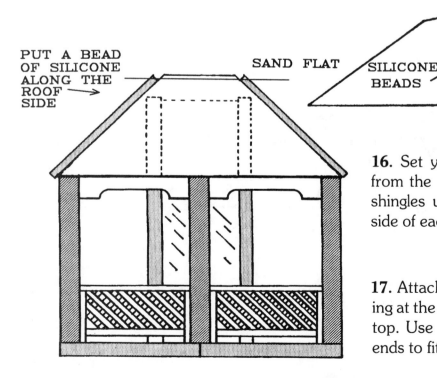

PUT A BEAD OF SILICONE ALONG THE ROOF SIDE

SAND FLAT

CUT AND TRIM TO FIT THE SHAPE OF THE ROOF

SILICONE BEADS

16. Set your band saw to cut a 3/16" width from the wood blocks you just cut. Slice the shingles using a push stick at the back and side of each wood piece.

17. Attach the wood shingles to the roof starting at the bottom and working your way to the top. Use ½" finishing nails and glue. Cut the ends to fit.

18. Measure and cut the roof top molding and the roof side or edge covers and glue and screw into position using 1″ screws. Use a heavy bead of silicone and cut off the excess after it dries.

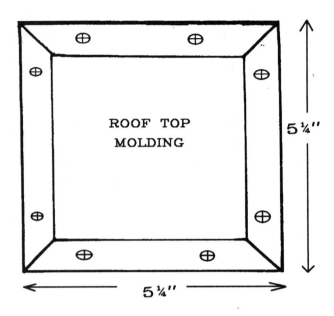

ROOF TOP
MOLDING

5¼″

5¼″

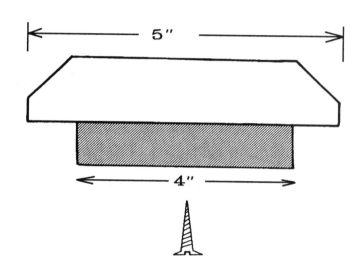

5″

4″

19. Measure and cut the two wood pieces forming the lid, center the smaller piece on the bottom of the larger and glue and screw into place. Optional: I cut a bevel in the top piece to conform with the slant of the roof.

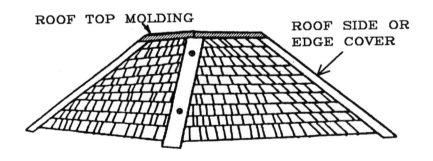

ROOF TOP MOLDING

ROOF SIDE OR
EDGE COVER

20. Finish the project with the paint or sealant of your choice, find a post and attach your classic one of a kind birdfeeder.

SEMI-SQUIRREL-PROOF FEEDER

Another name for this feeder could be bird selective feeder. That is, you determine the types of birds who use the feeder by modifying the size of the entrance hole. Nothing is totally squirrel proof but this project should deter them for awhile. This project is designed to be post mounted and allows for the seed to fall to the ground so the ground feeders can join the feast.

MATERIALS

¾" plywood, pressure-treated
1 piece 17" x 17" top
1 piece 16" x 16" base
1 piece 2½" diameter lid base
1 piece 7" hexagon lid bottom
1 piece 5" hexagon lid middle
1 piece 3" hexagon lid top

1x8 lumber pressure-treated
4 pieces ¾" x 12" feed chamber
4 pieces 3" x 20" post housing
4 pieces 4" x 5¾" perches
4 pieces 5¾" x 12" sides

HARDWARE AND MISCELLANEOUS

36 screws 1½" Dacrotized
4 pieces acrylic ⅛" x 4" x 11½"
    feed chamber walls
4 pieces acrylic ⅛" x 8" x 11½"
    feeder sides
Silicone glue
8 wire brads 1"
1 screw 3"

TOOLS REQUIRED

Drill with countersink bit
    and 2½" hole cutter
Screwdriver
Hammer
Sabre or band saw
Table saw
Tri-square
Web clamp or rope

DIRECTIONS

1. Measure and cut the boards for the post housing from the 1x8 wood stock. Cut a 2" quarter circle in the end of each board. Cut two ¾" slots 1½" deep in each board so that they overlap each other and form a 3⅝" opening to fit the post.

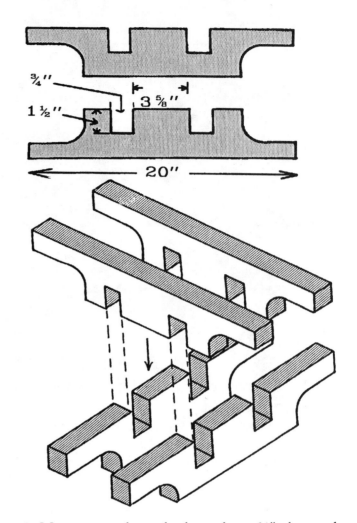

2. Measure and cut the base from ¾" plywood. It is a 16" hexagon with four opposite sides cut to 6" and four 8¼". Center and attach to the top of the post housing using 1½" screws and glue.

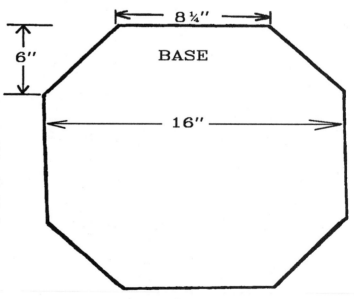

3. Measure and cut the top. It is a 17″ hexagon with four opposite sides cut to 6¼″ and four 8″. Cut a 2½″ circle from the center with a sabre saw or hole cutter. Save the cut-out piece to be added to the lid.

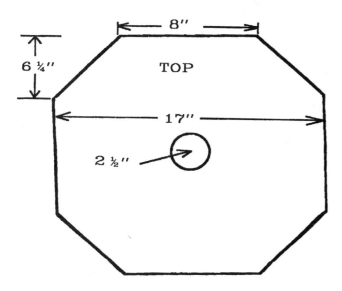

4. Measure and cut the four sides from the 1x8 wood stock, 5¾″ x 12″. Cut a 45-degree dado or slot ¼″ deep and ½″ from each edge ⅛″ wide (saw kerf). Cut an entrance hole 1¾″ as shown, ¾″ from the bottom of each side board.

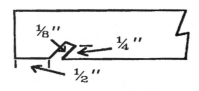

5. Measure and cut the four pieces of acrylic material for the sides 8″ x 11½″. Assemble the side boards and the acrylic sheets using silicone glue. Make certain the pieces are flush at one end leaving a ½″ gap at the other end. Use a web clamp or tie a rope around the assembly to keep it secure until the glue sets up.

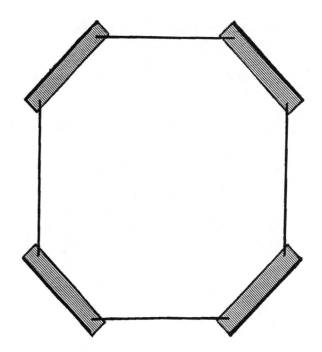

6. Measure and cut the boards for the feed chamber. They are 12″ long, ¾″ x ¾″. Cut a ⅛″ wide dado ¼″ deep into the center of two sides as shown.

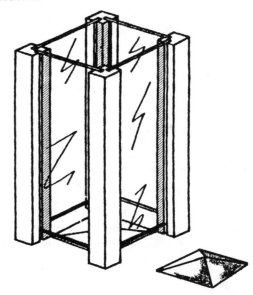

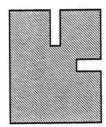

7. Measure and cut the four acrylic sheets that form the feed chamber walls, 4″ x 11½″.

8. Assemble the feed chamber pieces and glue. Allow to dry thoroughly.

9. Glue and toenail the feed chamber in the center of the base using 1″ wire brads. Option: at this point you may wish to cut a small pyramid piece to fit at the bottom center of the feed chamber. This will cause the feed to roll to the outside of the chamber. Cut a square 3½″ with a 1″ rise for this purpose and glue it in place.

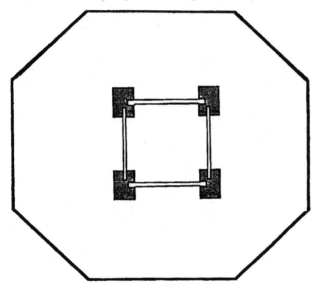

10. Center and attach the assembly from step 6 to the base with 1½″ wood screws. Make certain the opening is on the bottom. Attach the top to this assembly and to the feed chamber using 1½″ screws. Don't forget to use glue.

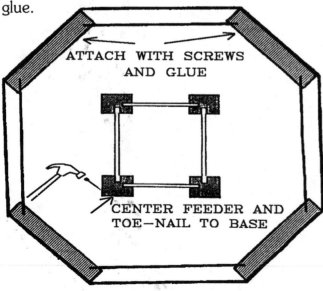

ATTACH WITH SCREWS AND GLUE

CENTER FEEDER AND TOE—NAIL TO BASE

11. Measure and cut the four perch pieces from the 1x8 wood stock, 4″ x 5¾″. Attach to the front of each entrance hole using glue and 1½″ screws.

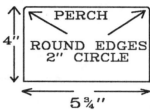

PERCH
4″ ROUND EDGES
2″ CIRCLE
5¾″

12. Measure and cut the pieces that form the lid from ¾″ plywood. Center all pieces one on top of the other and glue and screw together using 1 screw 3″ long.

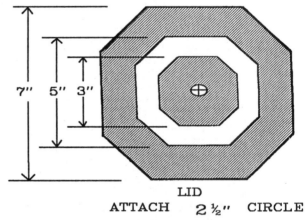

7″ 5″ 3″

LID
ATTACH 2½″ CIRCLE
TO BOTTOM

1¾″

ALLOW ½″ GAP SO
SEED CAN FALL TO THE GROUND

THE SWEETHEART BIRDFEEDER

This beautiful feeder is a welcome addition to anyone's back yard. The heart motif plus the Swedish peasant painting makes this a very special project indeed. You can omit the decorative painting, and this is still a great looking project. We used heart redwood which weathers to a dull grey over time.

MATERIALS

1x12 redwood (actual width 11")
1 piece 11" x 12½" back
1 piece 11" x 7" floor
1 piece 11" x 2" lip
1 piece 11" x 4¾" arch
2 pieces 8½" x 9¼" roof
2 pieces 8½" x 10" sides

HARDWARE AND MISCELLANEOUS

24 finishing nails #6
12 wire brads ¾" with heads
1 piece clear acrylic sheet
⅛" x 6" x 12"
1 piece flexible strip 2" x 9"
Silicone glue
Wood filler

TOOLS REQUIRED

Drill
Table saw or radial arm saw
Sabre saw or scroll saw
Hammer
Countersink

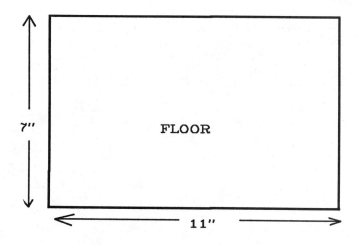

DIRECTIONS

1. Measure and cut the back, floor and lip from the full width stock.

2. Measure and cut the roof pieces. Tilt the saw blade to match the angle of the back. Ours was about 26 degrees.

3. Measure and cut the two side pieces. Tip: double up the stock and cut once to make certain you have matched pieces.

4. Draw the arch shape onto the redwood and cut to size. Drill a starter hole in the heart area and cut to shape with a sabre saw. This piece must be a perfect match with the top of the back piece. Take your time and draw the design onto the wood carefully.

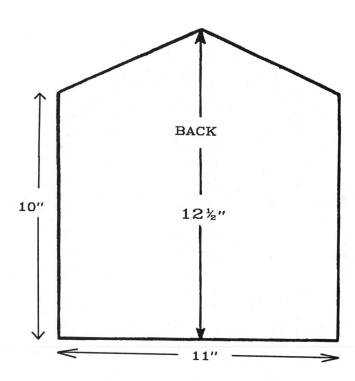

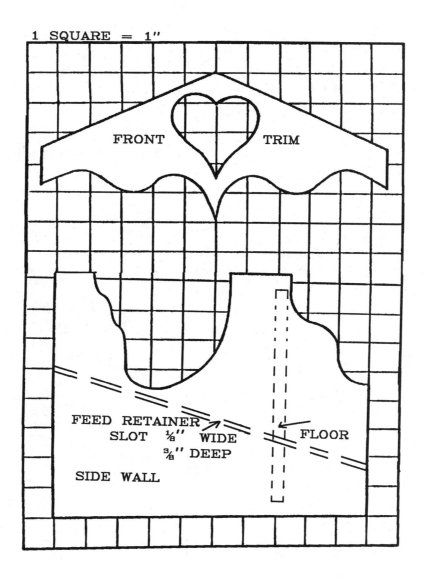

1 SQUARE = 1"

FRONT TRIM

FEED RETAINER
SLOT ⅛" WIDE
⅜" DEEP

FLOOR

SIDE WALL

5. Cut a ⅜" saw blade kerf into the inside of the two side pieces for the feed retainer as shown. Make certain the kerf is wide enough to accept the ⅛" acrylic sheet.

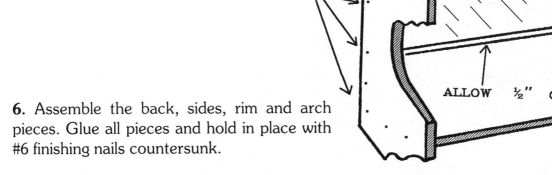

26°

NAIL

ALLOW ½" GAP

6. Assemble the back, sides, rim and arch pieces. Glue all pieces and hold in place with #6 finishing nails countersunk.

7. Measure and cut the clear acrylic sheet to size. Remove the protective backing and slip into place in the two slots cut in the side pieces. Hold in place with clear silicone glue. Make certain there is at least a ½" opening at the bottom for the seed to flow through.

8. Position, glue and nail the left roof side into place, recessing the nails. Attach the right roof piece to the left roof piece with the flexible strip and ¾" headed wire brads. Tip: you can cut the flexible strip from any plastic bottle. We used a milk bottle.

9. Seal the feeder with the wood sealer of your choice. Attach the feeder to the side of a building or a post. You are certain to foil the squirrels if you attach it to a metal building at least 5 feet from the ground.

MOUNT ON A POST OR THE SIDE OF AN EXTERIOR WALL

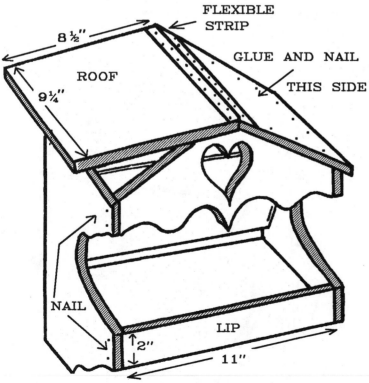

FLEXIBLE STRIP

GLUE AND NAIL

THIS SIDE

8 ½"

ROOF

9¼"

NAIL

LIP

2"

11"

THE COUNTRY STORE FEEDER

This project brings back memories of an age gone past, when lollipops were only a penny and the pace was slower. Even if you don't paint it, this replica of a little country store is certain to catch the attention of everyone. This project is designed to be post mounted and holds over 5 lbs. of birdseed.

MATERIALS

¾" plywood, pressure-treated
1 piece 6" x 12" front roof
1 piece 6½" x 12" back roof
1 piece 11" x 12" store front
1 piece 7¾" x 10½" back
1 piece 11" x 12" base
2 pieces 6" x 9½" sides

1x4 lumber, pressure-treated
2 pieces ⅛" x 1" x 12" trim
2 pieces ⅛" x 1" x 5" trim
4 pieces ⅛" x ½" x 3⅛" window trim
4 pieces ⅛" x ½" x 4⅝" window trim
2 pieces ¾" x ¾" x 6½" porch posts
1 piece 1½" x 10¼" feed tilt

¼" plywood
1 piece 5¼" x 10¼" feed tilt board
1 piece 1¾" x 5¾" door

HARDWARE AND MISCELLANEOUS

20 screws 1½" Dacrotized
20 screws ¾" flathead zinc coated
Silicone glue
2 pieces acrylic 3½" x 4" windows
1 strip flexible material, 1½" x 12"
   roof hinge
30 wire brads ¾"

TOOLS REQUIRED

Drill with countersink bit
Screwdriver
Radial arm saw or table saw
Sabre saw or coping saw
Hammer

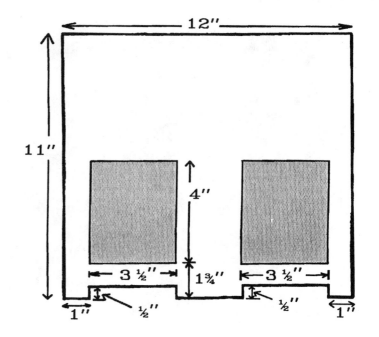

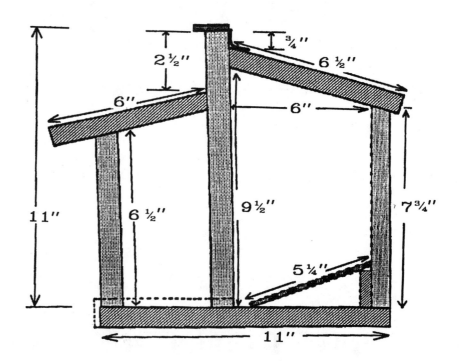

DIRECTIONS

1. Measure and cut all of the pieces from the ¾" pressure-treated plywood. Drill a starter hole in the store front for the windows and cut to size with a sabre saw or coping saw.

2. Measure and cut the acrylic sheet to fit the window openings.

3. Measure and cut all of the trim pieces and the front posts from the ¾″ wood stock.

4. Glue and nail the window trim pieces in place allowing for a ¼″ overhang around the window opening. Run a ⅛″ bead of silicone glue around the inside of the window openings and against the back of the trim. Insert the acrylic windows into this glue and allow to let dry thoroughly.

5. Assemble the floor, sides, front and back, and glue and screw together. Remember to countersink the screws.

6. Measure and cut the feed tilt board from the ¼″ plywood. Cut the other feed tilt board from the 1″ wood stock. Glue the 1″ stock across the inside back of the feeder chamber. Place the ¼″ feed tilt board on top of this board and glue and nail in place with ¾″ wire brads. Run a bead of silicone around the sides and back of the ¼″ tilt board so no seed can slip underneath.

7. Measure and cut the front and back roof pieces from the ¾″ plywood stock. Cut the part that fits against the store front and back to a 15-degree angle.

8. Attach the front roof and posts using glue and 1½″ screws to the porch area. Attach the back roof with a flexible hinge using silicone glue and ¾″ flathead coated wood screws. Tip: cut the hinge from a discarded plastic milk carton.

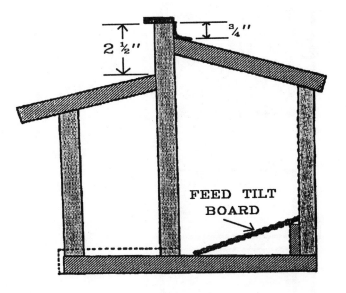

9. Measure and cut the door from ¼″ plywood and tack in place using glue and ¾″ wire brads.

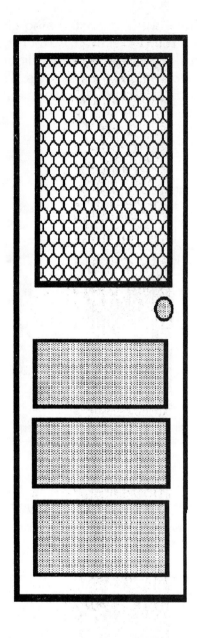

10. Measure and cut the trim pieces from the 1″ wood stock. Attach one 12″ strip to the top of the store front and one to the front. Put the two 5″ strips on the side of the porch forming a ledge to minimize seed spills to the ground. Use ¾″ wire brads and glue.

11. Paint the feeder the color of your choice or stain it with a good preservative.

12. Go find a post, fill the feeder with seed and put an open sign on the store front porch.

THE RED DOG SALOON FEEDER

Put a little of the old wild west in your back yard. Actually even if you don't paint it, it still makes a great conversation piece, and it does a terrific job of dispensing birdseed. This project is designed to be post mounted or it could be put on a railing in a corner of your deck or patio.

MATERIALS

¾″ plywood, pressure-treated
1 piece 4″ x 12″ front roof
1 piece 9½″ x 12″ back roof
1 piece 3″ x 12″ saloon sign
1 piece 12″ x 12¾″ base
2 pieces 7¼″ x 9″ sides
1 piece 7¾″ x 12″ back
1 piece 9¼″ x 12″ front

1x4 lumber, pressure-treated
2 pieces ¾″ x ¾″ x 10″
    front roof supports (posts)
1 piece ⅛″ x 1″ x 12″ trim
4 pieces ⅛″ x 1″ x 6″ trim
2 pieces ⅛″ x 1″ x 3½″
    trim
1 piece ⅛″ x 3″ x 3″ doors
1 piece 1½″ x 10″ feed tilt

¼″ plywood
1 piece 7¼″ x 10⅜″ feed
    tray

HARDWARE AND MISCELLANEOUS

2 pieces clear acrylic ⅛″ x
    3⅝″ x 3⅝″ windows
24 screws 1½″ Dacrotized
20 wire brads ¾″
2 hinges ½″ x 2″ with
    plated screws
Silicone glue
4 finishing nails 1½″
Wood filler

TOOLS REQUIRED

Drill with countersink bit
Sabre saw or coping saw
Screwdriver
Hammer
Circular saw or table saw
Bandsaw

DIRECTIONS

1. Measure and cut all of the wood pieces from the ¾″ plywood. One end of both the front and back and two roof pieces are cut at a 12-degree angle.

2. Measure and cut the two front posts, the feed tilt board and all of the trim and door pieces from the 1x4 lumber stock. This is best done with a band saw.

3. Measure and cut the openings in the front piece for the windows and the feed openings. The cutouts for the windows are 3⅝″ square. The feed area is ¾″ x 3⅝″.

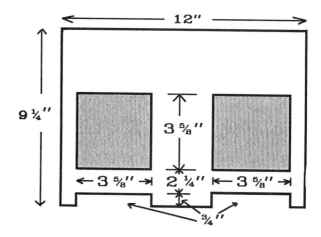

4. Assemble the front, back and side pieces using glue and 1½″ wood screws. Use the countersink. Attach this assembly to the base.

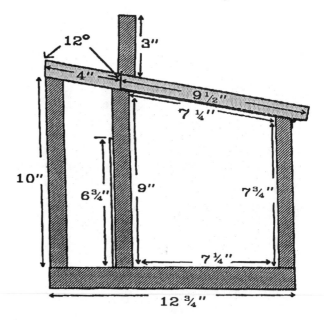

5. Attach the trim pieces to the front using glue and ¾″ wire brads. Allow a ¼″ overlap of the window edges.

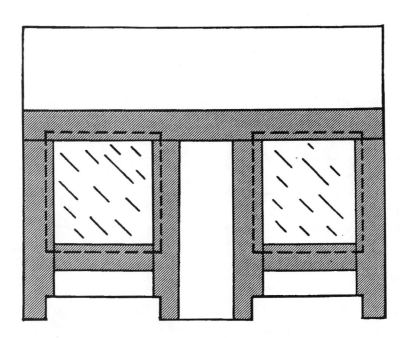

6. Measure and cut the two windows from the ⅛″ acrylic. Run a ⅛″ bead of silicone glue around the inside of the window and window trim. Remove the acrylic sheet backing and press the two pieces into place and into the bead of glue. Allow the glue to set up before proceeding.

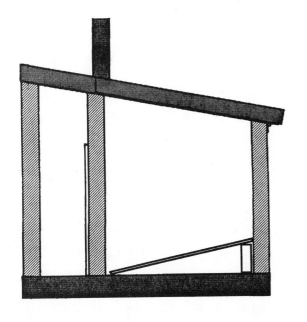

7. Measure and cut the feed tray from the ¼″ plywood stock. Glue the feed tilt board and the feed tray inside of the feed chamber so that the seed will flow forward to the seed dispenser openings in the front. Tack in place with ¾″ wire brads. Run a bead of silicone around the edge of the sides and back of the feed tray so the seed cannot fall underneath.

8. Attach the front roof and the posts using glue and 1½″ screws. Note that the front roof only overlaps half of the top of the front board. Use 1½″ finishing nails to attach the roof here. Countersink the screws for the posts or they may split otherwise.

10. Measure and cut the swing door mock up to size using ⅛″ wood stock. Note: you could also substitute ¼″ plywood. Paint the fake louvers on the door and attach it to the front of the saloon using ¾″ wire brads and glue.

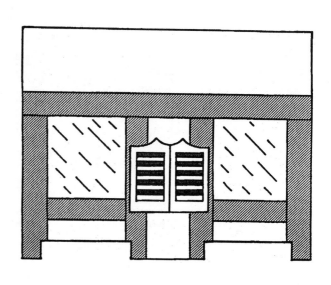

9. Attach the sign board to the front of the rear roof and attach this assembly to the top of the feed chamber using hinges at the underneath back.

11. Fill all nail holes and the sides of the plywood with wood filler. Let the filler dry, then paint the finished feeder the color of your choice.

MULTISTATION POST FEEDER

This unusual feeder holds a lot of birdseed. It can be used in many different ways. You could integrate it with a line of fence or patio wind shield, or just put it in the middle of the yard. One thing is certain, it's bound to get some comments from the neighbors. You can tell when it is time for a seed refill as the birds begin congregating only at the lower level stations. This is a surprisingly simple feeder to construct.

MATERIALS

1x8 lumber, pressure-treated
2 pieces 5" x 8' sides
2 pieces 3½" x 8' sides
12 pieces 2¼" x 4" roof
12 pieces 2¼" x 3¼" roof
1 piece 2¾" x 2¾" lid base

2x6 lumber, pressure-treated
1 piece 5" x 5" lid
1 piece 3½" x 3½" feed tilt
12 pieces 1¾" x 4" feed control

HARDWARE AND MISCELLANEOUS

48 screws 1½" Dacrotized
24 screws 3" Dacrotized
24 screws 2½" Dacrotized
Silicone glue

TOOLS REQUIRED

Circular saw
Drill with countersink and 1" bits

DIRECTIONS

1. Measure and cut the side boards. Rip from 1x8 material. Two sides are 3½" wide and two 5" wide, all boards are 8 feet long.

2. Measure and cut the feed tilt chamber board from 2x6 stock. The size is 3½" square with a bevel to two outside edges. Cut the bevel so there is a 1½" peak at the center beveling to ½" at the sides or edges.

3. Position and drill the 1" feed holes into the four side boards as shown.

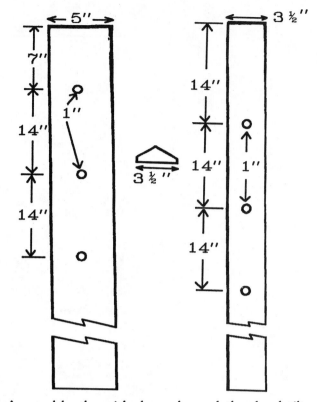

4. Assemble the side boards and the feed tilt board and put the main post together with 1½" screws. Countersink the screws and use silicone glue to seal the edges thoroughly. Put the feed tilt at the bottom feed hole and position it so the lip of the tilt board is at the bottom of the hole in the post and forces the seed to flow outward. Caulk the edges of the tilt board with silicone so no seed can slip past.

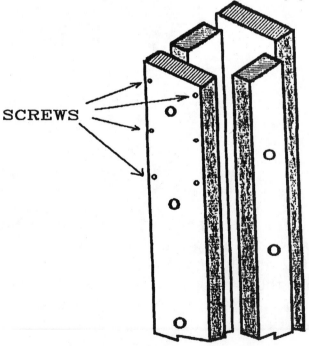

SCREWS

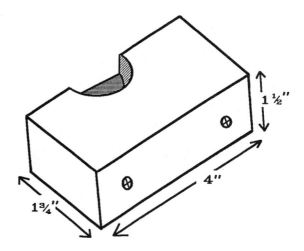

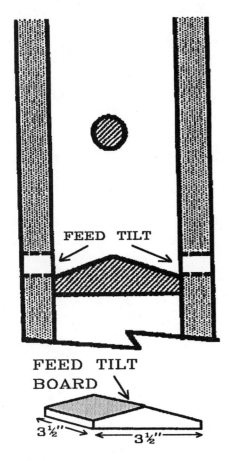

FEED TILT

FEED TILT BOARD

3½" 3½"

5. Measure and cut the roof pieces and assemble with 1½" screws and glue.

7. Position the feed control boards so that the bottom of the 1" hole is centered at the bottom of the 1" hole drilled in the post. Attach the boards with two screws 2½" long and glue. Countersink the screws.

8. Position the roof assemblies 4 to 5 inches above the feed control board. Attach to the post using 3" screws and glue.

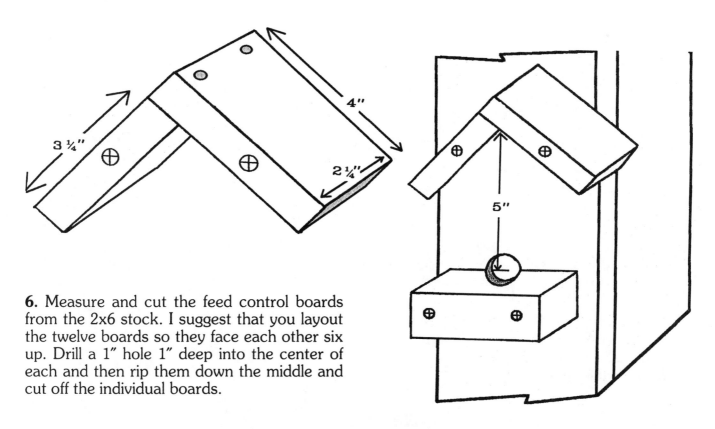

4"

3¼"

2¼"

5"

6. Measure and cut the feed control boards from the 2x6 stock. I suggest that you layout the twelve boards so they face each other six up. Drill a 1" hole 1" deep into the center of each and then rip them down the middle and cut off the individual boards.

9. Measure and cut the lid from 2x6 stock. It is 5″ square with a slight bevel at the top (optional). Cut the lid bottom from 1″ stock and center and glue and screw to the bottom of the lid with a 1½″ screw.

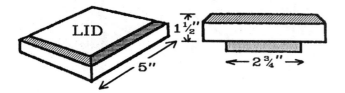

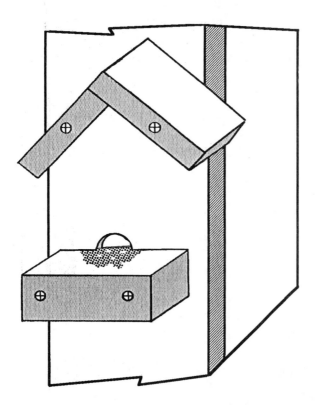

10. Seal the project with a good exterior grade sealer. You can then paint it or decorate it as we did with a vines-and-roses motif.

11. Dig a post hole 30″ to 36″ deep and plant the post feeder. Make certain it is level. Fill it with birdseed, put the lid on and stand back and watch the crowd gather.

FLYING SAUCER FEEDER

This feeder is made from a 2 liter soda bottle and some scrap lumber. It looks a little weird but it really does a great job of dispensing the birdseed and it is an extremely simple project to make. This is a good project for children and parents to work on together.

MATERIALS

¾″ plywood, pressure-treated
1 piece 8½″ diameter feed tray
1 piece 4¼″ diameter base

HARDWARE AND MISCELLANEOUS

1 plastic soda bottle 2 liter
1 piece wood strip (optional)
　1/16″ x 1″ x 27⅝″ rim
1 stove bolt 3/16″ x 2″ with
　washer, nut and lock washer
Silicone glue
8 wire brads ¾″

TOOLS REQUIRED

Drill with ¼″ bit
Sabre saw or coping saw
Screwdriver
Needle nose pliers
Razor knife

DIRECTIONS

1. Fill the 2 liter soda bottle with hot tap water to clean the interior and to soften the glue holding the base on. Remove the base by twisting it off when the glue softens. Clean off all excess glue.

2. Using a razor knife cut two ⅝″ holes on opposite sides in the neck of the bottle near the rim as shown.

3. Measure and cut the feed tray from the ¾″ plywood. Center and draw the inner circle. Drill a starter hole with a ¼″ drill bit and then cut out the inner circle. Trim the inner circle to 4¼″. Drill a ¼″ hole in the center.

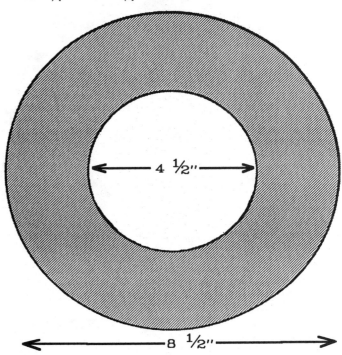

4　½″

8　½″

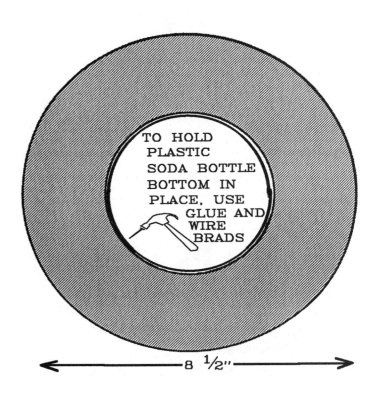

TO HOLD
PLASTIC
SODA BOTTLE
BOTTOM IN
PLACE, USE
GLUE AND
WIRE
BRADS

8　½″

4. Drill a hole in the center of the bottle cap and the bottle base. Using a 3/16" stove bolt assemble the bottle cap, inner circle and base. Take care not to crack the bottle cap.

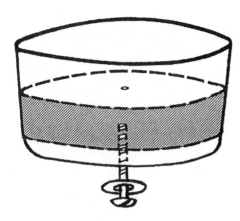

5. Using clear silicone glue, attach the above assembly to the inner circle of the feed tray. Allow to dry thoroughly. Put a small bead of glue around the bottle cap so that it stays in place on the inner circle.

6. To minimize the seed spillage put a rim around the feed tray. Cut a 1" wide strip of wood 1/16" thick and 27⅝" long. Attach to the feed tray using wire brads and glue.

7. Fill the bottle with a small size birdseed. You will need to use a funnel to do this properly.

8. Attach the bottle to the feed tray assembly by screwing it into the bottle cap. Go find a post, mount your feeder and watch the crowd gather.

SWISS CHALET BIRDFEEDER

This upscale version of a Swiss chalet is certain to stop people in their tracks when they see it in your yard. This is one of our more sophisticated designs and takes about 35 hours of effort in the shop to put it all together. This is one project that is certainly worth the effort to make since it will be talked about for years.

MATERIALS

¾" plywood, pressure-treated
1 piece 16" x 16" feeder base
1 piece 16½" x 19½" second level
2 pieces 16½" x 13" triangle, second level
2 pieces 18½" x 21" roof

½" plywood, pressure-treated
2 pieces 8½" x 11¼" seed enclosure

2x4 lumber, pressure-treated
4 pieces 16" long cut to shape, base
 support
8 pieces 1⅛" x 1⅛" x 10½" columns

2x10 lumber, pressure-treated
110 pieces ⅛" x 1¼" x 9" shingles
2 pieces ¾" x 5" triangle,
 chimney support
4 pieces 1" x 18½" roof trim
1 piece 5½" x 11¼" feed
 dispenser base, second level
56 pieces ⅛" x 1" x 3" tulip shaped
 fence slats, first level
28 pieces ⅛" x 1" x 2½" tulip shaped
 fence slats, second level
8 pieces ⅛" x 1" x 2½" tulip shaped
 slats, shutters
8 pieces ½" x 1½" x 7" cut to shape,
 valances

1" lumber, pressure-treated
2 pieces ¾" x ¾" x 16" and 2 pieces
 17½" long, base trim
16 pieces ½" x ½" x 7" banisters, first level
4 pieces ½" x ½" x 2½" and 2 pieces
 7¾" banisters, second level
4 pieces ¾" x ¾" x 4½" second level
 banister posts,
4 pieces ¾" x ¾" x 10½" slotted with
 ⅛" groove ¼" deep, feed dispenser,
 lower level
16 pieces ¼" x ¼" strips cut to size,
 window trim, second level (approximately
 2⅜" and 2⅝" long)
2 pieces ¼" x ¾" x 2½" and 2 pieces
 10¾" long, roof peak trim

⅛" thermoplastic sheeting
4 pieces 4½" x 10" feed dispenser,
 lower level
2 pieces 2⅜" x 2⅝" windows, upper level

4x4 post, pressure-treated
1 piece 10" long cut to shape,
 chimney

HARDWARE AND MISCELLANEOUS

5 tubes silicone glue
60 screws 1½" Dacrotized or
 galvanized
4 screws 2½" Dacrotized or
 galvanized
Box ½" wire brads galvanized
Box ¾" wire brads galvanized

TOOLS REQUIRED

Band saw
Table saw or radial arm saw
Sabre saw
Drill, 1" and 2½" hole cutters
Screwdriver
Hammer

1. Measure and cut the 16" x 16" base from ¾" plywood stock. We recommend you use Wolmanized™ Extra Pressure-Treated Lumber. It is treated for water resistance and will hold up much longer than other pressure-treated products.

2. Rip the base side pieces from 1" lumber stock. Attach them to the sides of the base using 1½" screws and silicone glue.

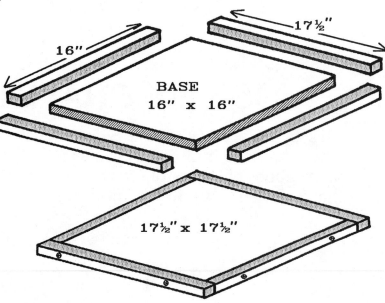

3. Rip the columns from 2x4 stock. The size is 1⅛″ square, 10½″ long.

4. Pre-drill a recessed screw hole in the bottom of the base for each column. Position and attach the columns using 1½″ screws and silicone glue.

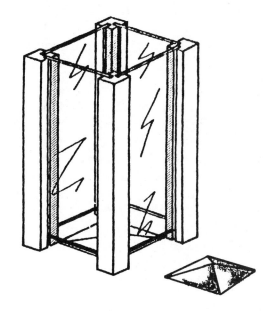

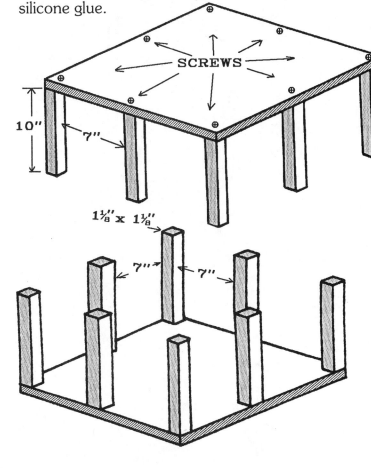

1⅛″ x 1⅛″

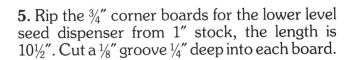

5. Rip the ¾″ corner boards for the lower level seed dispenser from 1″ stock, the length is 10½″. Cut a ⅛″ groove ¼″ deep into each board.

6. Measure and cut the ⅛″ thermoplastic sides 4½″ x 10″.

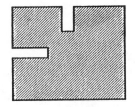

7. Position and glue the corner blocks and the thermoplastic sheets together with clear silicone glue. Make certain there is at least a ½″ gap at the bottom so the seed will pour onto the base properly.

8. Center the assembly from above on the base and glue and nail in place using ¾″ galvanized wire brads. The seed will flow to the outside of the dispenser better if you place a low level (1″ high 4″ square) wood pyramid in the center of the dispenser.

9. Measure and cut the base for the second level from ¾″ pressure-treated lumber. Cut the sides to conform to the roof angle of 60 degrees. The base measurement is 19½″ x 17½″ with cut outs as shown. The angle will make the measurement of the top of the base 16½″ wide. The bottom, which fits on top of the columns, is 17½″ wide.

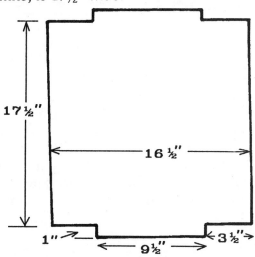

10. Pre-drill recessed screw holes for attachment of the second level to the columns. Position the second level on top of the columns and attach using 1½″ screws and silicone glue.

11. Measure and cut the triangular-shaped sides of the second level from ¾″ pressure-treated plywood. The size is 16½″ at the base to a peak of 13″ in the center top. Center the measurement for the window, drill a starter hole and cut to size using a sabre saw. Cut the opening at the bottom for the seed to flow onto the second level balcony. This opening is 5½″ wide and ¾″ deep. Note: if you plan to use a lot of large seed such as sunflower seed you may want to make this opening 1″.

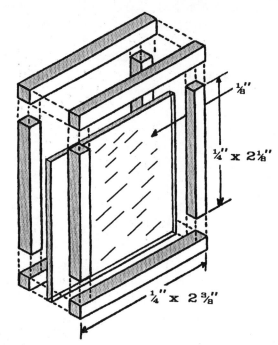

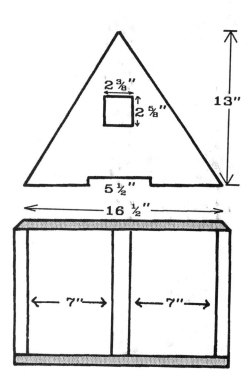

13. Measure and cut the second level seed container sides from ½″ pressure-treated lumber. The size is 8½″ x 11¼″. Cut the top side at a 60-degree angle to match the roof pitch.

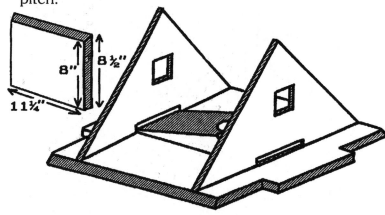

14. Measure and cut the second level feed dispenser base from 2x10 pressure-treated lumber, 5½″ x 11¼″, 1½″ thick at the center and slanted to ¼″ at each end so the feed will flow towards the opening.

12. Cut ¼″ square stock from the pressure-treated 1″ lumber and cut strips to frame the inside of the window. Glue in place. Cut the ⅛″ thermoplastic to size and sandwich with another frame of strips. Again glue in place. Allow the glue to dry before proceeding.

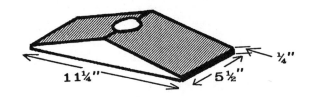

15. Position, center the feed dispenser base on top of the second floor, glue and screw in place with 1½″ Dacrotized or aluminum screws and let dry thoroughly.

16. Center and drill a 2½″ hole down through the feed dispenser base and through the second floor. This can also be done with a sabre saw. This will allow the birdseed to flow into the bottom dispenser.

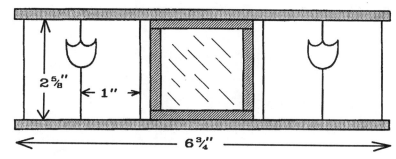

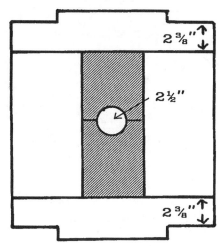

17. Position the triangular sides and the sides of the second level feed dispenser flush against the sloping dispenser base and attach all pieces with silicone glue and 1½″ screws. Toe-nail the triangular pieces to the roof with ¾″ nails and silicone glue. Run glue around the inside of the feeder assembly to seal the cracks so seed cannot slip into any potential future openings.

18. Measure, cut and assemble the second story window pieces as shown. Attach to the triangular-shaped boards. To make tulip slats, follow the procedure in steps 19 through 21 for the rail slats.

19. The tulip slats that make up the decorative feature of the fence and rail system are cut from 2″ pressure-treated lumber stock. The bottom level slats are 1″ x 3″ and the top pieces 1″ x 2½″. The only safe way to make these pieces is with either a band saw or scroll saw. First cut the blank stock for each size shown. Next cut ½ of each tulip design as shown. Set the fence on your band saw to ⅛″ and slice the pieces from the stock. You will need 56 pieces for the first level and 28 for the second level. Make certain the wood grain goes from top to bottom.

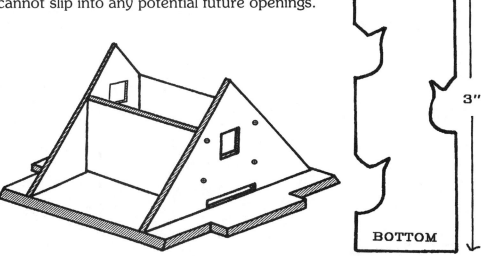

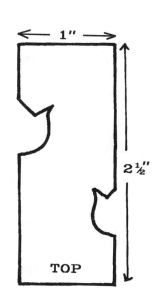

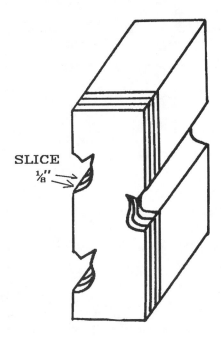

SLICE
1/8"

20. Rip ½" square stock from the 1" pressure-treated lumber. Cut a ⅛" slot in the center of these strips ¼" deep. Cut the strips slightly longer than 7" for the first level and 11" for the second level.

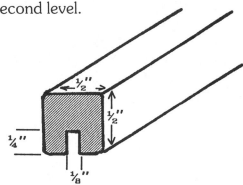

½"

½"

¼"

⅛"

21. Using silicone glue assemble the rails and slats by reversing every other slat to form the tulip design. Insert the slats into the ⅛" groove in the rails. Allow to dry overnight.

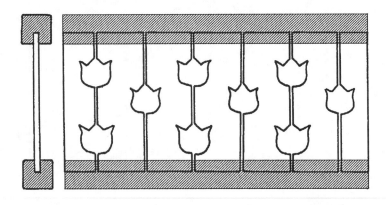

22. Cut the lower level slat and rail assemblies to fit the openings between the columns. We suggest you do this one at a time. Allow a ½" opening at the bottom and maintain this uniformly around the lower level. Attach the assemblies to the center of the columns with silicone glue and ¾" aluminum or galvanized wire brads.

23. Measure and cut the second level posts from 1" pressure-treated lumber. Cut the four posts ¾" square and 4½" long.

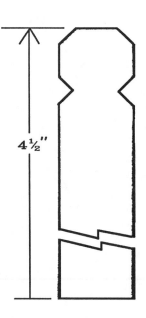

4½"

24. Assemble the second level banister and posts by cutting each front piece of the rail and slat assembly to 7¾" for the front and two pieces 2½" for the sides. Attach the rail and post pieces to the post using silicone glue and ¾" aluminum or galvanized wire brads. Remember to allow a ½" opening or gap at the bottom. Allow this assembly to dry thoroughly and then attach to the second level using silicone glue and ¾" aluminum or galvanized wire brads.

25. Trace the design for the valances onto 2" wood stock and cut to shape. Adjust the fence of your band saw to ½" and slice the valance pieces from the 2" stock. Make 8 valances.

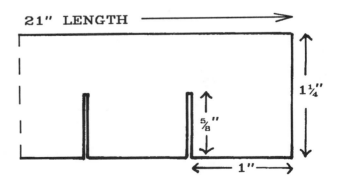

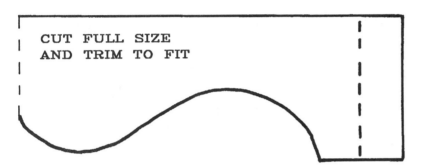

CUT FULL SIZE
AND TRIM TO FIT

26. Cut each valance to length to fit the openings at the top of the columns. We suggest you do this one at a time. Using silicone glue and ¾" aluminum or galvanized nails attach the valances in the center of each column over the rail and slat assembly.

27. Measure and cut the two roof pieces from ¾" pressure-treated plywood. The size is 18½" x 21". The edge that forms the peak of the roof is cut at a 30-degree angle.

28. Attach the roof to the top of the triangular shaped boards with silicone glue and 1½" screws. Allow a 1" overlap at each end.

29. Cut an opening to form the feed entrance at the peak of the roof 5" from one end, 3⅝" wide and 3" down the side of the roof. This will house the chimney assembly which will also cover the feed entrance.

30. The roof shingles can be purchased at most craft stores or stores selling doll house kits. We suggest however that you make your own from pressure-treated lumber. Cut 1¼" strips from the ends of a 2x10. Using a table saw or a radial arm saw, cut ⅛" saw kerfs ⅝" deep at 1" intervals. Set the fence of your band saw to ⅛" width and slice off the strips that form the shingles. You will need 110 strips.

21" LENGTH

1¼"

⅝"

1"

31. Attach the shingles to the roof using silicone glue and ½" galvanized finishing nails. Start by running a strip of shingles with about a ⅛" overlap at the bottom of the roof edge. Follow with a row of shingles with the slots in the center of each previous shingle about ¼" from the tip of the first row of shingles. The next row should start with the edge of the shingle at the end of the saw kerf, ⅝" from the tip of the previous shingle layer. Remember to position the saw kerf in each shingle to fall in the center of each preceding shingle. This will allow for a smooth run off of rain water.

32. Measure and cut the chimney piece 10" long from a 4x4 pressure-treated post. Cut the lower end to shape. Using a table saw, radial saw or router, cut the grooves to form the brick effect. I used a table saw to cut the horizontal slots and cut the vertical slots with a chisel.

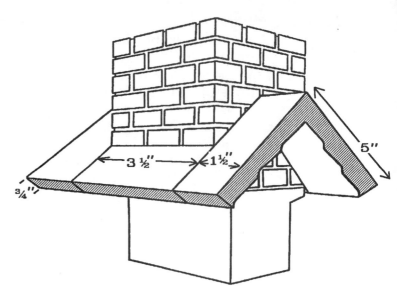

34. Measure and cut the roof peak trim pieces from 1" stock. Cut two pieces 2½" long and two pieces 10¾" long. Attach to the roof peak with ¾" galvanized wire brads and silicone glue.

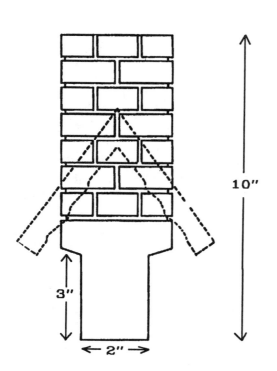

33. Measure and cut the chimney supports to size. Make two. Cut two center support pieces. Assemble the chimney and support pieces using silicone glue. Allow this assembly to dry thoroughly.

35. This step is optional. Cut ¾" strips ¼" thick to cover the side grain of the plywood on the roof and second floor. Measure and cut to length and attach using ¾" galvanized wire brads and silicone glue.

36. Measure and cut the base support boards from 2x4 pressure-treated lumber, cut to 16" lengths. Cut slots 1½" wide and 1¾" deep as shown so the boards can interlock forming a center designed to fit over a 4x4 post. Center on the bottom of the base and attach using four 2½" Dacrotized or galvanized screws.

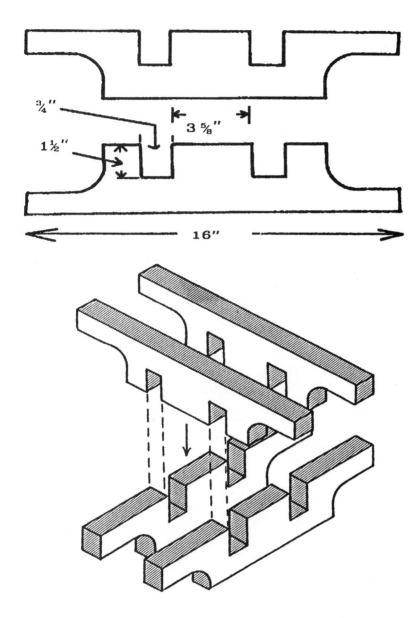

¾"

3 ⅝"

1½"

16"

37. Seal the outside of the feeder with a good brand of water seal.

38. Attach to a 4x4 post anchored in concrete.

39. Fill with your favorite birdseed, attach the chimney and shout "Soups On." Sit back and watch the flocks of birds zero in on your masterpiece of a diner.

ROOSTING BOX

Roosting boxes are just the opposite of birdhouses. Where birdhouses need to be well ventilated, roosting houses must be sealed tightly to keep out the cold winter wind. This design with heart cutouts says you care. The birds will welcome this cozy resting place where they can congregate in the winter months.

MATERIALS

1x12 pine
1 piece 5½" x 10" gable
1 piece 9⅞" x 10" door
1 piece 10" x 16" back
1 piece 8½" x 10" base
2 pieces 7½" x 11¾" sides
1 piece 5" x 24" back board
1 piece 8½" x 9½" roof
1 piece 7¾" x 9½" roof

2x4 pine
1 piece 1½" x 1½" x 4"
   chimney

HARDWARE AND MISCELLANEOUS

2 hinges ¾"x 2" brass
1 hook and eye screw small
24 screws 1½" Dacrotized
4 pieces ¼" plywood 4" x 4"
   heart decorations
4 wood dowels ¼" x 7" perches
Small can wood filler
12 wire brads ¾"
Silicone glue

TOOLS REQUIRED

Drill with countersink bit,
   ¼" bit and 1¾" spade bit
Circular saw
Sabre saw

DIRECTIONS

1. Measure and cut the back, base and side boards from the 1x12 wood stock. Remember to cut the top of each side board to a 45-degree angle.

2. Assemble the above pieces with screws and glue.

3. Measure and cut the two roof pieces and assemble with glue and screws. Let dry thoroughly.

4. Measure and cut the four perches from ¼" wood dowel. The length should be 8".

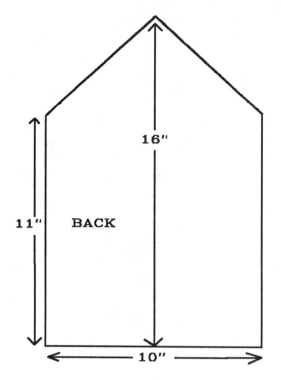

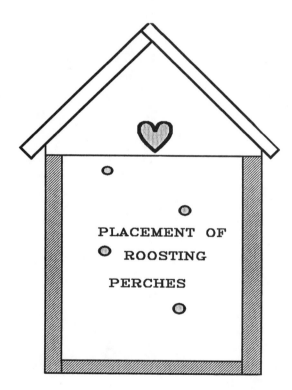

5. Drill four staggered holes in the back. Position the holes so that there is enough room between the perches for the birds' headroom. Depending on the size bird you want this project to house, you may only need two or three perches. Use glue to attach perches.

6. Attach the roof using screws and glue. Countersink the screw holes.

7. Measure and cut the gable and attach to the upper front part of the roosting box. Use glue and screws.

8. Measure and cut the door. Drill a 1¾" opening hole in the lower right or left of the door about 1" from the bottom. If you plan to use the heart decoration pieces, it would be advisable to cut them to shape and attach one on the door before drilling the opening.

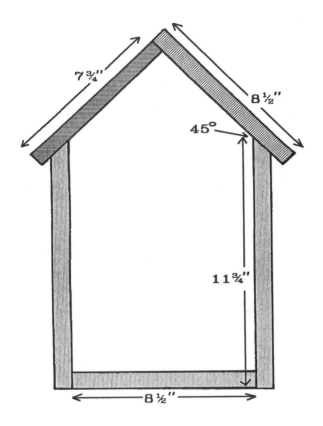

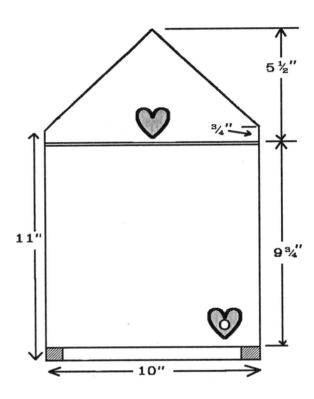

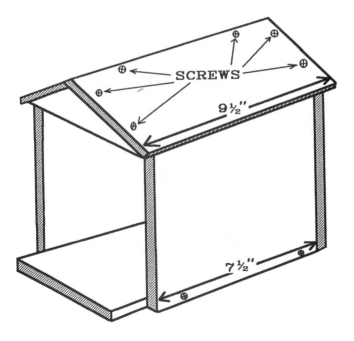

9. Attach the door to the front using 2" brass hinges. Attach a hook-and-eye screw on the other side. Make certain the door closes tightly. Each spring it will be necessary to clean out the roosting box and readjust the hook so the door stays secure and tight to minimize drafts.

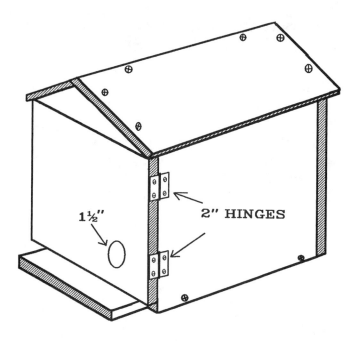

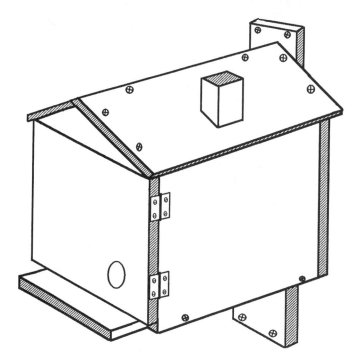

10. Draw the heart decorating pieces onto ¼″ plywood and cut to shape. Glue and nail into position on the side and front of the roosting box. Use ¾″ wire brads and glue.

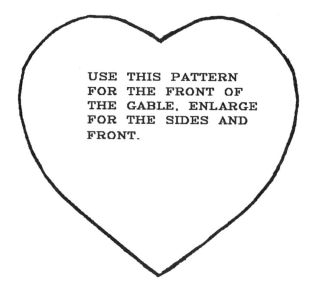

USE THIS PATTERN FOR THE FRONT OF THE GABLE. ENLARGE FOR THE SIDES AND FRONT.

11. Measure and cut the back board and attach to the center of the back. Pre-drill screw holes at the top and bottom.

12. Measure and cut the chimney from 2x4 stock. It is 1½″ square and 4″ long. Cut a 45-degree miter at one end. Attach the chimney to the roof using a 1½″ screw and glue.

13. Go over the whole project with wood filler, filling over all countersunk screw holes and any cracks or nicks in the wood surface. Sand flush.

14. Seal the project with a suitable exterior-grade wood sealer. Paint the project the color of your choice.

15. Install the roosting box in a tall tree facing away from the North wind. You could also install it in the upper eaves of your house away from any traffic zone.

ONE VARIATION OF A ROOSTING BOX

RAIN COVER WINDOW FEEDER

This feeder has an extensive tray feeding area that is covered by a sheet of acrylic. It affords the birds protection from the elements and at the same time dispenses food. This feeder will hold about 5 lbs. of birdseed. If you use a tinted acrylic, it will lessen the likelihood of the birds being able to see you observing them.

MATERIALS

1x8 lumber, pressure-treated
2 pieces 7" x 24" sides
1 piece 7" x 17" back
2 pieces 4" x 6½" x 2" feed
    chamber sides
1 piece ¾" x 17" top trim
1 piece 1½" x 17" bottom trim
1 piece 5" x 18¼" lid top
1 piece 3" x 15¼" lid bottom
1 piece 9" long tray support

½" plywood, pressure-treated
1 piece 18" x 21" feed tray

⅛" acrylic sheeting
1 piece 6½" x 16¼" feed
    chamber front
1 piece 17⅝" x 12" feed
    tray cover

HARDWARE AND MISCELLANEOUS

1 piece wood dowel ⅜" x 18½" perch
2 screws 1¼" Dacrotized
12 screws 1½" Dacrotized
16 finishing nails 1" galvanized
Silicone glue

TOOLS REQUIRED

Drill with ⅜" bit and countersink bit
Table saw
Hammer
Sabre saw or band saw

DIRECTIONS

1. Measure and cut the feeder sides. You can approximate the shape of the front. To maintain uniformity in the shapes, cut the front of both pieces simultaneously.

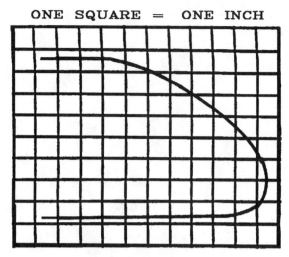

ONE SQUARE = ONE INCH

2. Measure and cut the back, the top and bottom trim pieces.

3. Measure and cut the tray from ½" plywood. The size is 18" x 21".

4. Cut a ⅛" slot in the inside top of the feeder side boards ¼" from the edge and ⅜" deep.

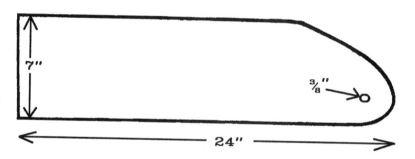

5. Next cut a ½" dado on the inside bottom of the feeder side boards as shown. Do the same to the back board.

6. Cut a ⅜" wood dowel for the perch to a length of 18½". Assemble the sides, back, bottom and perch using glue, 1½" screws for the back and 1" finishing nails on the bottom.

7. Measure and cut the feed chamber walls from the 1x8 wood stock. Cut a ⅛" slot ⅜" deep ¼" from the slanted edge as shown.

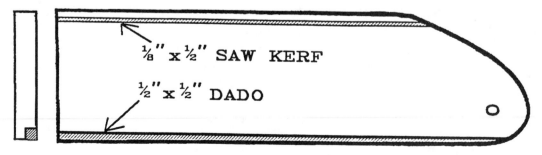

⅛" x ½" SAW KERF

½" x ½" DADO

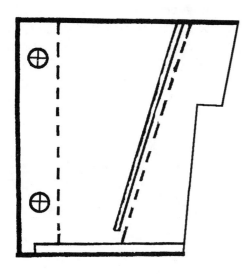

9. Measure and cut the top and bottom boards that form the lid. Center the bottom board under the lid board and glue and screw in place using two 1¼" screws.

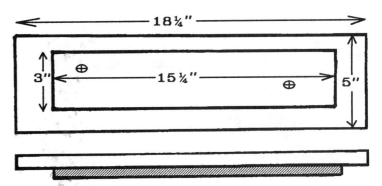

10. Measure and cut the tray support board. The shape we used is shown; however, you only need a board 3" wide with two 5-degree cuts on each end. You will have to experiment with this step as the shape of your window and the wall will be the ultimate determining factor.

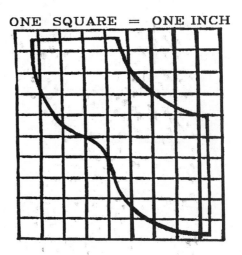

ONE SQUARE = ONE INCH

SAW KERF ⅛"

8. Measure and cut the feed chamber front from the ⅛" acrylic sheet. The size is 6½" x 16¼". Assemble and install the feed chamber in the back of the feeder as shown. Hold the sides in place with 1½" wood screws and the acrylic in place with silicone glue. Make certain there is a ½" opening at the bottom for the feed to pour through. Allow the glue to dry before proceeding.

11. Attach the feeder to your window using three 1½" screws through the bottom back of the feed chamber into your window sill. Attach the support board to the feeder, holding it level. Use two 1½" screws.

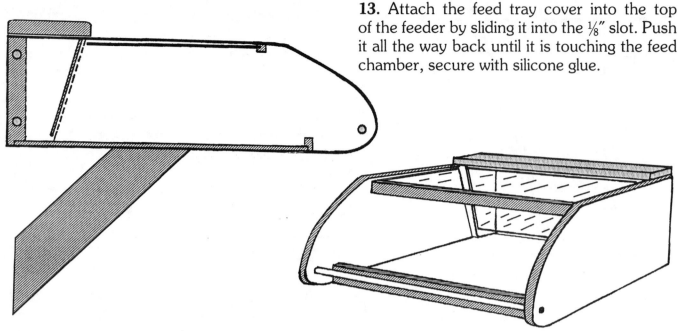

13. Attach the feed tray cover into the top of the feeder by sliding it into the ⅛″ slot. Push it all the way back until it is touching the feed chamber, secure with silicone glue.

12. Cut a ⅛″ slot as shown in the top trim piece. Cut a ½″ dado in the bottom trim piece. Cut the acrylic feed tray cover to size, 12″ x 17⅝″.

14. Attach the top and bottom trim pieces with glue and screws.

15. Fill the feeder with seed and put the top in place.

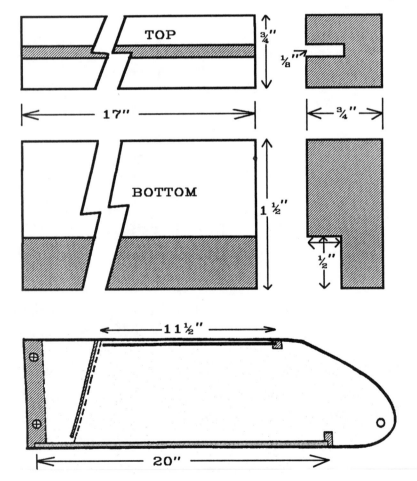

THE SWEETHEART WINDOW FEEDER

This is a great weekend workshop project for everybody in the family. With one exception, all of the wood cuts are very basic. I used a router to soften the edges of the heart shape and the lid but you could omit these steps and sand them instead. This feeder is designed to bring the birds right to your window sill, but it is best used with a window that has a protective overhang to keep the seed dry in rainy weather.

MATERIALS

1x8 lumber, pressure-treated
1 piece 7¼″ x 27½″ tray
2 pieces ¼″ x 1″ x 28″ trim
2 pieces ¼″ x 1″ x 7¼″ trim
2 pieces 4″ x 8″ x 7″ sides
1 piece 7¼″ x 7¼″ lid
1 piece 5½″ x 6″ lid bottom
1 piece 7¼″ x 9″ support

⅛″ acrylic sheet
2 pieces 6½″ x 7¼″ feeder sides
2 pieces 4″ x 4¾″ heart cover

HARDWARE AND MISCELLANEOUS

8 screws ⅝″ brass
4 screws 1½″ Dacrotized
24 finishing nails 1″ galvanized
Silicone glue
Assorted sandpaper

TOOLS REQUIRED

Sabre saw
Hammer
Drill with ½″ bit and countersink bit
Table saw
Router with rounding over bit
2 c-clamps 2″

DIRECTIONS

1. Measure and cut the feed tray from 1x8 wood stock. 1x8 lumber actually measures ¾″ x 7¼″ to 7½″.

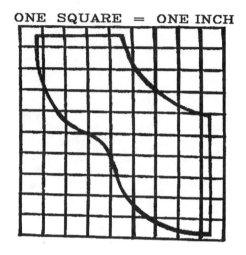

ONE SQUARE = ONE INCH

2. Rip the tray trim. Attach the trim to the tray using glue and 1″ finishing nails.

3. Draw the tray support form onto a 9″ length of 1x8. Note: this design is optional. All you need is a 45-degree cut on two sides of a straight board to support the bottom of the tray against the side of the house. Cut to shape.

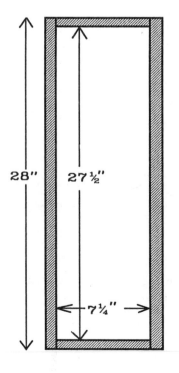

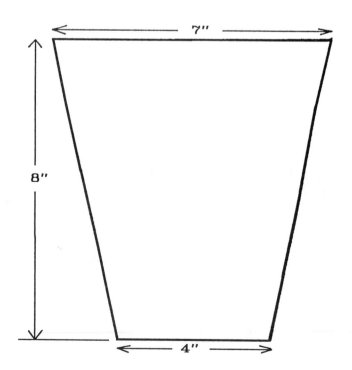

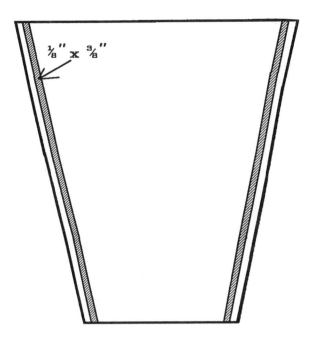

1/8" x 3/8"

4. Measure and cut the feed chamber sides from 1x8 wood stock. Using a table saw, cut a 1/8" wide groove 3/8" deep into the sides 1/4" from each edge as shown.

6. Cut two pieces of 1/8" acrylic sheet to cover the heart cut outs. Attach to the sides on the side with the slot, using 5/8" brass screws. Countersink the holes in the acrylic and be careful as it breaks easily.

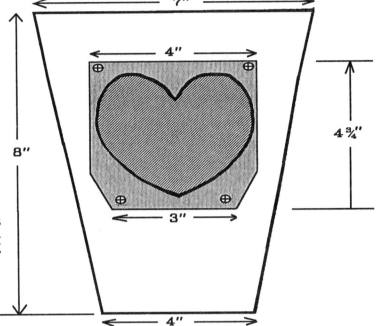

7"

4"

8"

4 3/4"

3"

4"

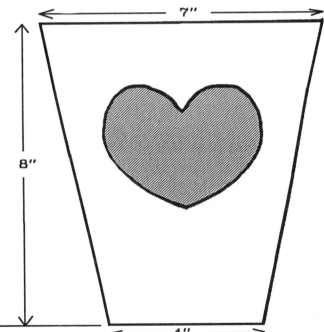

7"

8"

4"

5. Draw the heart shape onto the sides and cut to shape using a sabre saw.

7. Cut the remaining acrylic sides to size. Assemble the feed chamber by gluing the acrylic into the slots in the wood sides. Clamp lightly and allow to dry thoroughly. Be certain to glue the acrylic flush with the top of the wood sides. There should be a 1/2" gap at the bottom.

6 1/2"

7 1/4"

8. Measure and cut the lid and the lid bottom from 1x8 wood stock. Assemble the lid pieces with glue and two 1½″ screws.

9. Using a router with a rounding over bit, rout the lid top. If you wish, the heart shapes can also be routed on the outside but this must be done before the acrylic is in place.

10. Attach the feed tray to your window ledge with 1½″ screws. Position the support so that the tray is level, attach to the tray bottom with two 1½″ screws.

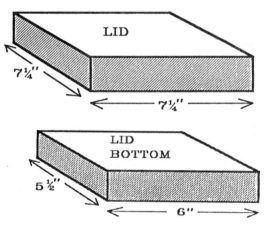

11. Position the feed chamber on top of the tray. If you wish attach it with two screws from the bottom of the tray. Fill with seed and attach the lid.

12. Position yourself near the inside of the window and watch the customers line up.

PIE-TIN BIRDBATH

Take an ordinary 9" pie tin and some lumber and "presto" you've got a great looking birdbath. This project would look good in anybody's back yard. The birds will repay your kindness by keeping your yard free of flying insects. You in-turn will be entertained by their splashing and pruning as they take advantage of the free bath.

MATERIALS

1x4 lumber, pressure-treated
4 pieces 3" x 16" post frame
8 pieces 2¾" x 7½" sides

½" plywood, pressure-treated
1 piece 18" octagon top

HARDWARE AND MISCELLANEOUS

24 finishing nails 1" galvanized
1 pie pan 9" aluminum or coated tin
Silicone glue
8 screws 1½" Dacrotized
Wood filler

TOOLS REQUIRED

Drill with ½" bit
Router with rounding over bit
Table saw
Sabre saw
Circular saw
Web clamp
Nail set
Hammer

DIRECTIONS

1. Measure and cut the eight-sided top from ½" pressure-treated plywood.

2. Draw a circle in the center of the top large enough to hold the pie pan but narrow enough to catch it at the rim.

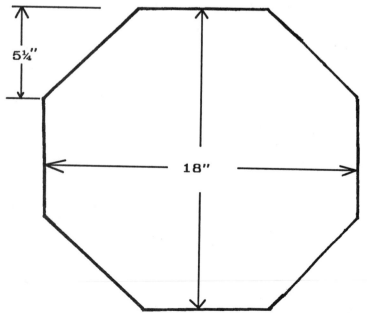

3. Drill a ½" starter hole and cut the circle to shape using a sabre saw.

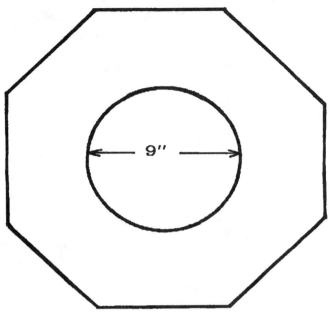

4. Measure and cut the four boards that form the post cap. Cut the slots as shown so the boards fit together forming a cap to put at the top of a 4x4 post.

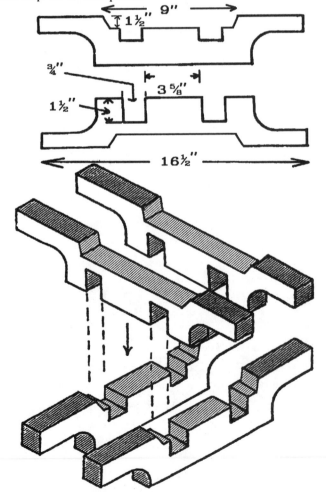

5. Rip the side board piece to 2¾" width. Adjust your saw to cut a ½" dado in one side.

6. Adjust your saw to cut a 22.5-degree miter. Cut the eight side boards to size (7½"). Make certain the dado is on the inside cut of each piece.

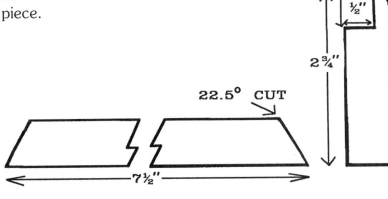

22.5° CUT

½"

2¾"

7½"

7. On a flat surface, assemble the eight sides. Glue all edges and form the octagon, pushing each piece close together. Using a web clamp, pull the assembly tight. Allow to dry thoroughly.

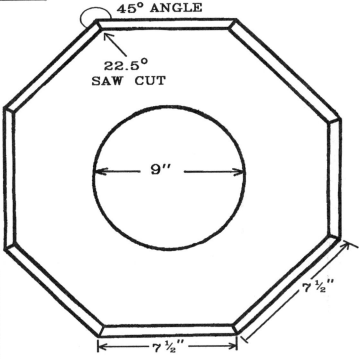

45° ANGLE

22.5°
SAW CUT

9"

7½"

7½"

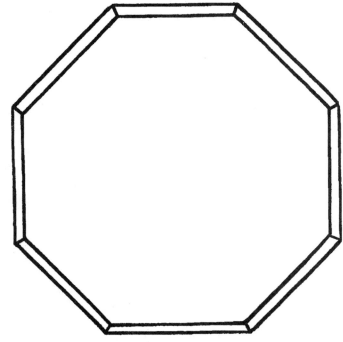

8. Toenail two finishing nails into the sides of each of the eight pieces. Recess with a nail set.

9. Attach the top to the side assembly using glue and 1" finishing nails. Recess the nails with a nail set.

10. Using a router with a rounding over bit, rout the edge of the birdbath to give it a softer and smoother look.

11. Attach the above assembly to the post cap using 1½" screws.

12. Attach the finished birdbath to the top of a 4x4 post about 36" to 48" off the ground. Add the pie tin and water and wait for the bathing to begin.

FEEDER AND WATERING HOLE COMBINATION

This project not only feeds the birds, it also provides them with water. When it has been properly installed, the pie tin holds the water and serves as a lid over the feed chamber. You can make several variations on this one design using the same basic concept.

MATERIALS

1x8 lumber, pressure-treated
2 pieces 11½" feeder sides
2 pieces 13" feeder sides
2 pieces ¼" x ½" x 18" trim
2 pieces ¼" x ½" x 18½" trim
4 pieces 2½" x 19" seed retainer walls
4 pieces 3" x 16" base support

½" plywood, pressure-treated
2 pieces 18" x 18" top and base

HARDWARE AND MISCELLANEOUS

16 screws 1½" Dacrotized
 8 screws 1¼" Dacrotized
18 wire brads ¾" galvanized
18 finishing nails 1" galvanized
Silicone glue
1 pie pan 9" aluminum or coated tin

TOOLS REQUIRED

Sabre saw
Drill with countersink and ½" bit
Table saw
Circular saw
Hammer
Screwdriver

DIRECTIONS

1. Measure and cut the top and base pieces from ½" plywood stock.

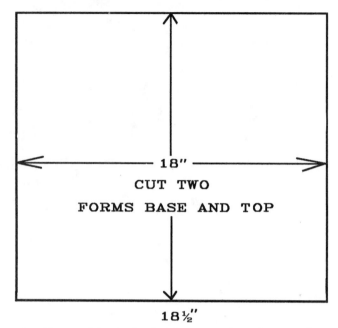

2. Cut a 9" circle in the center of one piece. Drill a starter hole with the ½" bit and cut to size with a sabre saw. Please double check the size of the pie pan. You want the hole large enough for the pan to fit with the lip resting on the plywood.

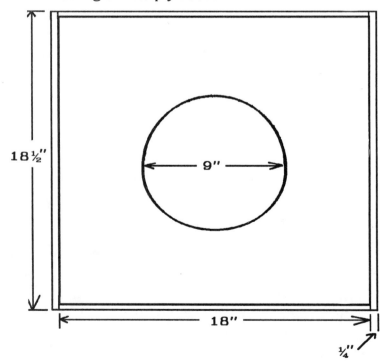

3. Measure and cut the trim for the top from 1x8 wood stock. The size is ¼″ x ½″ cut to the length necessary to trim the top as shown. Attach the trim to the top using ¾″ wire brads and glue, trim flush.

4. Measure and cut the seed retainer walls from 1x8 wood stock. The width is 2¾″ mitered to a length of 19″. Cut a dado ⅜″ x ¾″ in the top of each of the four boards.

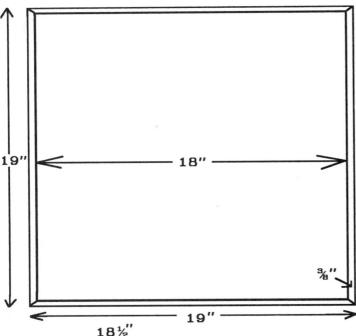

5. Attach the feed retainer walls to the base board using glue and 1″ nails.

6. Cut the feed chamber sides from 1x8 wood stock. Cut to the length specified. Using a sabre saw, cut the feed outlets as shown.

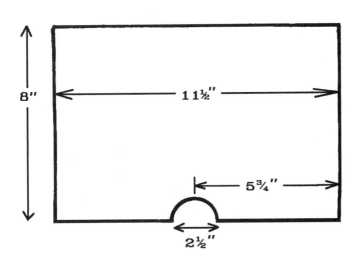

7. Assemble the feeder sides to form a 13″ square. Attach the boards with glue and 1½″ screws.

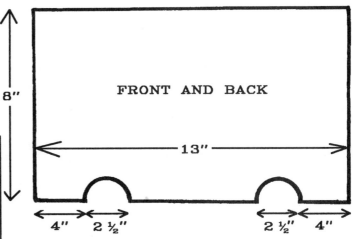

FRONT AND BACK

8. Center the feed chamber on the base assembly and attach with glue and 1¼″ screws. Center the top on this assembly and attach using glue and 1¼″ screws.

9. Measure and cut the base support pieces from the 1x8 wood stock. Cut the notches as shown so the boards fit together to form a support for the base and for attachment to a 4x4 post.

10. Run a small even bead of silicone glue around the bottom of the lip of the pie pan. Allow this to cure until it is semisoft. Attach the pie pan to the top and push down gently. This should cause the silicone to form a gasket around the opening thus making the top waterproof so rain water cannot get into the seed chamber.

11. Seal the project with a clear sealer.

12. Attach to the top of a 4x4 post, fill the feed chamber and the watering trough and await your guests.

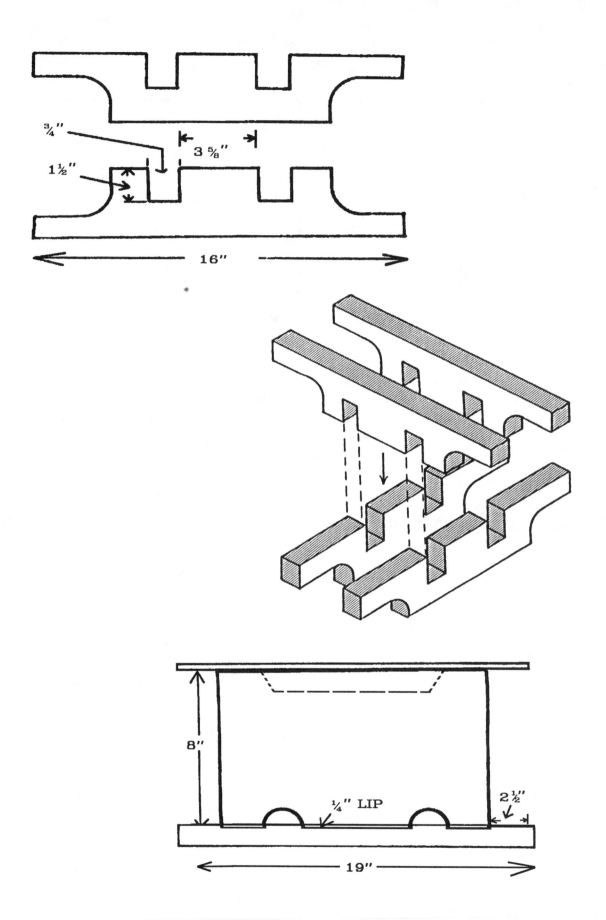

BIRDFEEDERS, SHELTERS & BATHS

FEEDER PROJECTS FOR LITTLE HANDS

Since I dedicated this book to my two small grandchildren, I thought it would be appropriate that we end it with some projects for little people. These simple but very useful projects can be easily made with the help of mom or dad or grandma and grandpa. It is important to decorate the humming bird feeder with a bright red bow to attract their attention. Woodpeckers will love the peanut butter log. The see-through feeder lets you see who's having lunch.

MATERIALS

See-through feeder

1x8 pine
2 pieces 7" x 8" sides
1 piece 7" x 8" bottom
1 piece 1½" x 9½" top
⅛" or 1/16" acrylic sheet
2 pieces 1½" x 9½" sides
2 pieces 4¼" x 9½" roof

Hummingbird feeder

1x4 pine 24" long
1 piece 3" x 6" back
2 pieces 4" x 4" sides
1 piece 3" x 3" bottom

Peanut butter log

2x2 pine 12" long

HARDWARE AND MISCELLANEOUS

12 finishing nails
   1" galvanized
2 screws 1½" Dacrotized
8 screws ⅝" brass
3 screw eyes small
1 half-pint milk carton
Silicone glue
Acrylic paint green, brown
   and red
1" paint brush
1 cup hook small
1 red ribbon small
Small can wood filler
Assorted sandpaper

TOOLS REQUIRED

Drill with countersink bit, ½" bit
   and 1" spade bit
Coping saw or sabre saw
Hand saw
Hammer
Nail set
Screwdriver
Scribe
Vice
Ruler
Square

DIRECTIONS

See-through feeder

1. Measure and cut the wood sides, top and bottom onto 1x8 wood stock.

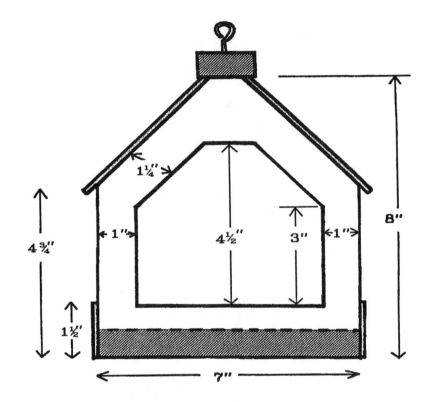

2. Drill a ½" starter hole into the cutout part of the wood sides. Using a coping saw or sabre saw cut out the opening.

3. Sand all of the edges of the wood pieces.

4. Position the bottom board between the two side boards and glue and nail together. Recess the nails with a nail set, fill the holes with wood filler and sand flush.

5. Drill a countersink hole into the center ends of the top piece and top of the ends. Position and glue and screw into place with 1½" screws.

6. Paint the project the color of your choice. We used brown paint for our sample.

7. Measure and cut the acrylic sheet; 1/16" will be easier for little hands to work with. The quickest way to do this is scribe the pieces and then snap them off.

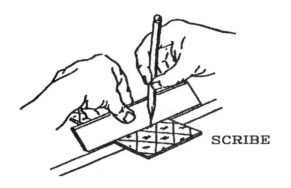

SCRIBE

10. Attach two small screw eyes at the top and go find a low-hanging branch to tie the feeder to with some nylon cord.

Hummingbird feeder

1. Measure and cut the sides, back and bottom from the 1″ wood stock.

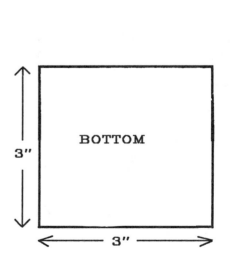

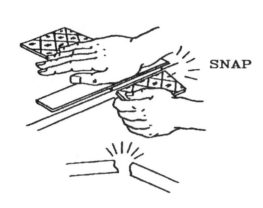

SNAP

8. Using a drill with a countersink bit, pre-drill the ends of all pieces.

9. Position the roof and side pieces and hold in place with ⅝″ screws. Drill starter holes with the countersink bit to make the screws go in easier.

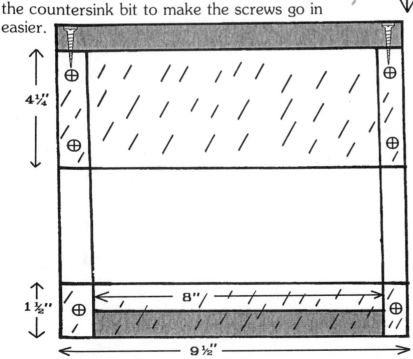

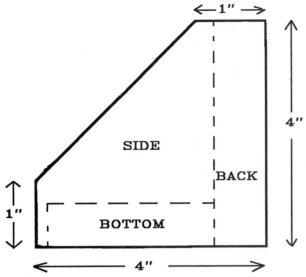

2. Position and glue and nail all of the pieces together. Recess the nails with a nail set and fill the holes with wood filler. Sand the project thoroughly.

3. With a countersink bit, drill a hole into the center top of the back piece.

4. Paint the whole project. We used green paint for our project.

5. Attach a small cup hook at the center of the top of the back board.

6. Tie a bright red ribbon to the cup hook.

7. Thoroughly wash out the milk carton. Glue a red or orange flower petal cut from some bright red construction paper or the side of a red plastic disposable bottle onto the side of the milk carton. Cut a small ½" hole into the center of the flower petal and milk carton.

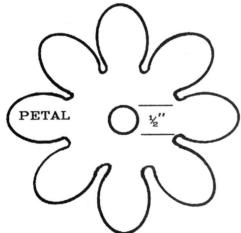

8. Fill the milk carton with sugar water. You can buy this at the store or make your own by mixing 1 part granulated sugar to 4 parts boiling water. Wait until the mixture cools before adding it to the feeder.

9. Put the feeder on the side of a building about 5 feet from the ground or higher. Make certain the flower petal is pointing outward. If you don't want to go to the trouble of making the feeder stand, you can just hang the milk carton from the limb of a tree.

Peanut butter log.

1. Cut a 12" length of 2x2. Do not sand it. In fact, the rougher it is the better.

2. Using a 1" bit, drill holes through the center of one side and top and bottom about 4" from each end of the other side.

3. Attach a small screw eye at the top.

4. Fill the holes with peanut butter and go find a branch to hang the project from. Use nylon cord to attach the project.

5. Go sit down on your back porch and wait for the crowd to arrive.

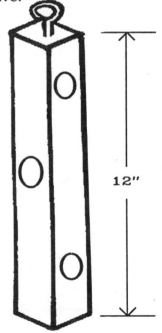